THE
G✝SPEL
IN YOU

**DISCOVER THE POWER
THAT CHANGES YOU
FROM THE INSIDE OUT**

PAUL CHAPPELL

Striving Together Publications
4020 E. Lancaster Blvd.
Lancaster, CA 93535
800.201.7748

Cover design by Andrew Jones
Writing assistance by Robert Byers

The contents of this book are the result of decades of
spiritual growth in life and ministry. It is not our intent
to claim originality with any quote or thought that could not
readily be tied to an original source.

ISBN 978-1-59894-457-0 (paperback)
ISBN 978-1-59894-458-7 (ebook)
Printed in the United States of America

TABLE OF CONTENTS

A NOTE FROM THE AUTHOR

I have had the privilege of preaching the amazing and powerful gospel of Jesus Christ for over forty years. And I *still* never tire of telling its story or of seeing the impact it has on a life.

The gospel is amazing and powerful. Romans 1:16 tells us it is the very "power of God unto salvation." But as incredible as that is, the work of the gospel in your life is not finished at the moment of your salvation; it is only beginning.

The gospel not only changes the destination of your eternal soul; it is the power that works in you *today* to change you from the inside out. The Bible tells us, "Therefore if any man be in Christ, he is a new creature: old things are passed away; behold, all things are become new" (2 Corinthians 5:17). The power of the gospel can change your relationships, priorities, aspirations, motives, witness…your entire life.

Unfortunately, many Christians are content to live simply with the gospel's assurance of eternal salvation but miss out on the gospel's ability for daily transformation and growth. The result is that their spiritual growth is severely stunted and they never gain victory over ongoing temptations or experience the inside-out transformation God desires to work in their lives.

This ninety-day devotional book is written to help you understand the significance of how profoundly the gospel can transform your life. It is for every Christian—from those who have just trusted Christ yesterday to those who have been saved for many years. After all, we are to be daily growing into the likeness of Christ through our entire Christian journey.

Each devotion in this book includes a Scripture passage and provides an encouraging or admonishing truth regarding the effect of the gospel in our lives. At the close of each devotion, you will find a single takeaway principle given as "The Gospel in You Today." Additionally, you'll find a Bible reading schedule at the bottom of each devotion that will lead you through the New Testament in ninety days.

I encourage you to read these devotions with your Bible open and your heart prepared to respond to God's truth. And I pray these devotions will encourage you to daily live for Christ through the power of the gospel that transforms you from the inside out.

Sincerely in Christ,
Paul Chappell

WHAT IS THE GOSPEL?

People use the word *gospel* in so many ways that there is tremendous value to clarifying what it means before you begin reading this book.

The word *gospel* simply means "good news." Throughout the New Testament, it refers to the best news of all: that Jesus died for your sin, was buried, and rose from the grave to offer you forgiveness—complete reconciliation with God—and the gift of eternal life.

This is how the apostle Paul defined the gospel in 1 Corinthians 15: "Moreover, brethren, I declare unto you the gospel which I preached unto you, which also ye have received, and wherein ye stand...For I delivered unto you first of all that which I also received, how that Christ died for our sins according to the scriptures; And that he was buried, and that he rose again the third day according to the scriptures" (1 Corinthians 15:1, 3–4). That *is* good news! Let's look at it more closely.

The Bible tells us in 1 John 5:13, "These things have I written unto you that believe on the name of the Son of God; that ye may know that ye have eternal life." How can you know that? Here it is in a nutshell.

Recognize Your Condition

Knowing Christ personally, starts with realizing that you are lost in sin. Romans 5:12 teaches us that since Adam and Eve, the first man and woman on Earth, a sin nature has been present in all people. Romans 3:23 says, "For all have sinned, and come short of the glory of God." Sin is any act contrary to God's laws and commandments, and those sins that we have committed separate us from God.

The Bible tells us that sin has a penalty. Romans 6:23 says, "For the wages of sin is death; but the gift of God is eternal life through Jesus Christ our Lord." The "wage" or payment for our sin is spiritual death—eternal separation from God.

Religion and Good Works Are Not the Answer

Religions try to create their own ways to God. Their systems may seem logical, but they cannot bridge the gap created by our sin. Proverbs 14:12 says, "There is a way which seemeth right unto a man, but the end thereof are the ways of death." In other words, our thoughts and ways are not what matter. God's Word, the Bible, provides true answers of grace and forgiveness. In Ephesians 2:8–9 the Bible says, "For by grace are ye saved through faith; and that not of yourselves: it is the gift of God: Not of works, lest any man should boast."

The Good News: Jesus Christ Provides the Way

Even though we were lost and separated from God, He loved us, and because He is love, God sent His Son to die on the cross and rise from the dead three days later. John 3:16 explains "For God so loved the world, that he gave his only begotten Son, that whosoever believeth in him should not perish, but have everlasting life." Through the death and resurrection of Jesus, He became the payment for our sin. Now, we do not have to pay for our sin ourselves. By His grace, salvation is provided. In Romans 5:8, the Bible says, "But God commendeth [meaning *proved* or *demonstrated*] his love toward us, in that, while we were yet sinners, Christ died for us."

Believe and Receive Christ

In order to have a relationship with God and an eternal home in Heaven, we must stop trusting ourselves, our works, and our religions, and place our full trust in Jesus Christ alone for the forgiveness of our sin and eternal life. In Romans 10:13 the Bible says, "For whosoever shall call upon the name of the

Lord shall be saved." That is a promise directly from God. If you will pray to Him, confess that you are a sinner, ask Him to forgive your sins, and turn to Him alone to be your Savior, He promises to save you and give you the free gift of eternal life. You can make that decision today by praying from your heart, something like this:

> Dear God, I know that I am separated from you because of sin. I confess that in my sin, I cannot save myself. Right now, I turn to you alone to be my Savior. I ask you to save me from the penalty of my sin, and I trust you to provide eternal life to me. Amen.

You'll never regret that decision. If you have just trusted Christ, send me an email at gospelinyou@strivingtogether.com to let me know. I would love to hear from you.

These truths—that Jesus died, was buried, and rose again for your sins and that He offers you forgiveness as a gift—constitute the gospel. After you believe the gospel and receive Christ, you can experience the life-changing power of the gospel to transform your daily living. This is because you now have the Holy Spirit within you. He wants to change so much more than your eternal destiny. He wants to transform *you*.

BIBLE
READING
SCHEDULES

ONE-YEAR BIBLE READING SCHEDULE

January

☐	1	Gen. 1–3	Matt. 1
☐	2	Gen. 4–6	Matt. 2
☐	3	Gen. 7–9	Matt. 3
☐	4	Gen. 10–12	Matt. 4
☐	5	Gen. 13–15	Matt. 5:1–26
☐	6	Gen. 16–17	Matt. 5:27–48
☐	7	Gen. 18–19	Matt. 6:1–18
☐	8	Gen. 20–22	Matt. 6:19–34
☐	9	Gen. 23–24	Matt. 7
☐	10	Gen. 25–26	Matt. 8:1–17
☐	11	Gen. 27–28	Matt. 8:18–34
☐	12	Gen. 29–30	Matt. 9:1–17
☐	13	Gen. 31–32	Matt. 9:18–38
☐	14	Gen. 33–35	Matt. 10:1–20
☐	15	Gen. 36–38	Matt. 10:21–42
☐	16	Gen. 39–40	Matt. 11
☐	17	Gen. 41–42	Matt. 12:1–23
☐	18	Gen. 43–45	Matt. 12:24–50
☐	19	Gen. 46–48	Matt. 13:1–30
☐	20	Gen. 49–50	Matt. 13:31–58
☐	21	Ex. 1–3	Matt. 14:1–21
☐	22	Ex. 4–6	Matt. 14:22–36
☐	23	Ex. 7–8	Matt. 15:1–20
☐	24	Ex. 9–11	Matt. 15:21–39
☐	25	Ex. 12–13	Matt. 16
☐	26	Ex. 14–15	Matt. 17
☐	27	Ex. 16–18	Matt. 18:1–20
☐	28	Ex. 19–20	Matt. 18:21–35
☐	29	Ex. 21–22	Matt. 19
☐	30	Ex. 23–24	Matt. 20:1–16
☐	31	Ex. 25–26	Matt. 20:17–34

February

☐	1	Ex. 27–28	Matt. 21:1–22
☐	2	Ex. 29–30	Matt. 21:23–46
☐	3	Ex. 31–33	Matt. 22:1–22
☐	4	Ex. 34–35	Matt. 22:23–46
☐	5	Ex. 36–38	Matt. 23:1–22
☐	6	Ex. 39–40	Matt. 23:23–39
☐	7	Lev. 1–3	Matt. 24:1–28
☐	8	Lev. 4–5	Matt. 24:29–51
☐	9	Lev. 6–7	Matt. 25:1–30
☐	10	Lev. 8–10	Matt. 25:31–46
☐	11	Lev. 11–12	Matt. 26:1–25
☐	12	Lev. 13	Matt. 26:26–50
☐	13	Lev. 14	Matt. 26:51–75
☐	14	Lev. 15–16	Matt. 27:1–26
☐	15	Lev. 17–18	Matt. 27:27–50
☐	16	Lev. 19–20	Matt. 27:51–66
☐	17	Lev. 21–22	Matt. 28
☐	18	Lev. 23–24	Mark 1:1–22
☐	19	Lev. 25	Mark 1:23–45
☐	20	Lev. 26–27	Mark 2
☐	21	Num. 1–2	Mark 3:1–19
☐	22	Num. 3–4	Mark 3:20–35
☐	23	Num. 5–6	Mark 4:1–20
☐	24	Num. 7–8	Mark 4:21–41
☐	25	Num. 9–11	Mark 5:1–20
☐	26	Num. 12–14	Mark 5:21–43
☐	27	Num. 15–16	Mark 6:1–29
☐	28	Num. 17–19	Mark 6:30–56

March

☐	1	Num. 20–22	Mark 7:1–13
☐	2	Num. 23–25	Mark 7:14–37
☐	3	Num. 26–28	Mark 8
☐	4	Num. 29–31	Mark 9:1–29
☐	5	Num. 32–34	Mark 9:30–50
☐	6	Num. 35–36	Mark 10:1–31
☐	7	Deut. 1–3	Mark 10:32–52
☐	8	Deut. 4–6	Mark 11:1–18
☐	9	Deut. 7–9	Mark 11:19–33
☐	10	Deut. 10–12	Mark 12:1–27
☐	11	Deut. 13–15	Mark 12:28–44
☐	12	Deut. 16–18	Mark 13:1–20
☐	13	Deut. 19–21	Mark 13:21–37
☐	14	Deut. 22–24	Mark 14:1–26
☐	15	Deut. 25–27	Mark 14:27–53
☐	16	Deut. 28–29	Mark 14:54–72
☐	17	Deut. 30–31	Mark 15:1–25
☐	18	Deut. 32–34	Mark 15:26–47
☐	19	Josh. 1–3	Mark 16
☐	20	Josh. 4–6	Luke 1:1–20
☐	21	Josh. 7–9	Luke 1:21–38
☐	22	Josh. 10–12	Luke 1:39–56
☐	23	Josh. 13–15	Luke 1:57–80
☐	24	Josh. 16–18	Luke 2:1–24
☐	25	Josh. 19–21	Luke 2:25–52
☐	26	Josh. 22–24	Luke 3
☐	27	Judges 1–3	Luke 4:1–30
☐	28	Judges 4–6	Luke 4:31–44
☐	29	Judges 7–8	Luke 5:1–16
☐	30	Judges 9–10	Luke 5:17–39
☐	31	Judges 11–12	Luke 6:1–26

April

☐	1	Judges 13–15	Luke 6:27–49
☐	2	Judges 16–18	Luke 7:1–30
☐	3	Judges 19–21	Luke 7:31–50
☐	4	Ruth 1–4	Luke 8:1–25
☐	5	1 Sam. 1–3	Luke 8:26–56
☐	6	1 Sam. 4–6	Luke 9:1–17
☐	7	1 Sam. 7–9	Luke 9:18–36
☐	8	1 Sam. 10–12	Luke 9:37–62
☐	9	1 Sam. 13–14	Luke 10:1–24
☐	10	1 Sam. 15–16	Luke 10:25–42
☐	11	1 Sam. 17–18	Luke 11:1–28
☐	12	1 Sam. 19–21	Luke 11:29–54
☐	13	1 Sam. 22–24	Luke 12:1–31
☐	14	1 Sam. 25–26	Luke 12:32–59
☐	15	1 Sam. 27–29	Luke 13:1–22
☐	16	1 Sam. 30–31	Luke 13:23–35
☐	17	2 Sam. 1–2	Luke 14:1–24
☐	18	2 Sam. 3–5	Luke 14:25–35
☐	19	2 Sam. 6–8	Luke 15:1–10
☐	20	2 Sam. 9–11	Luke 15:11–32
☐	21	2 Sam. 12–13	Luke 16
☐	22	2 Sam. 14–15	Luke 17:1–19
☐	23	2 Sam. 16–18	Luke 17:20–37
☐	24	2 Sam. 19–20	Luke 18:1–23
☐	25	2 Sam. 21–22	Luke 18:24–43
☐	26	2 Sam. 23–24	Luke 19:1–27
☐	27	1 Kings 1–2	Luke 19:28–48
☐	28	1 Kings 3–5	Luke 20:1–26
☐	29	1 Kings 6–7	Luke 20:27–47
☐	30	1 Kings 8–9	Luke 21:1–19

May

☐	1	1 Kings 10–11	Luke 21:20–38
☐	2	1 Kings 12–13	Luke 22:1–30
☐	3	1 Kings 14–15	Luke 22:31–46
☐	4	1 Kings 16–18	Luke 22:47–71
☐	5	1 Kings 19–20	Luke 23:1–25
☐	6	1 Kings 21–22	Luke 23:26–56
☐	7	2 Kings 1–3	Luke 24:1–35
☐	8	2 Kings 4–6	Luke 24:36–53
☐	9	2 Kings 7–9	John 1:1–28
☐	10	2 Kings 10–12	John 1:29–51
☐	11	2 Kings 13–14	John 2
☐	12	2 Kings 15–16	John 3:1–18
☐	13	2 Kings 17–18	John 3:19–36
☐	14	2 Kings 19–21	John 4:1–30
☐	15	2 Kings 22–23	John 4:31–54
☐	16	2 Kings 24–25	John 5:1–24
☐	17	1 Chr. 1–3	John 5:25–47
☐	18	1 Chr. 4–6	John 6:1–21
☐	19	1 Chr. 7–9	John 6:22–44
☐	20	1 Chr. 10–12	John 6:45–71
☐	21	1 Chr. 13–15	John 7:1–27
☐	22	1 Chr. 16–18	John 7:28–53
☐	23	1 Chr. 19–21	John 8:1–27
☐	24	1 Chr. 22–24	John 8:28–59
☐	25	1 Chr. 25–27	John 9:1–23
☐	26	1 Chr. 28–29	John 9:24–41
☐	27	2 Chr. 1–3	John 10:1–23
☐	28	2 Chr. 4–6	John 10:24–42
☐	29	2 Chr. 7–9	John 11:1–29
☐	30	2 Chr. 10–12	John 11:30–57
☐	31	2 Chr. 13–14	John 12:1–26

June

☐	1	2 Chr. 15–16	John 12:27–50
☐	2	2 Chr. 17–18	John 13:1–20
☐	3	2 Chr. 19–20	John 13:21–38
☐	4	2 Chr. 21–22	John 14
☐	5	2 Chr. 23–24	John 15
☐	6	2 Chr. 25–27	John 16
☐	7	2 Chr. 28–29	John 17
☐	8	2 Chr. 30–31	John 18:1–18
☐	9	2 Chr. 32–33	John 18:19–40
☐	10	2 Chr. 34–36	John 19:1–22
☐	11	Ezra 1–2	John 19:23–42
☐	12	Ezra 3–5	John 20
☐	13	Ezra 6–8	John 21
☐	14	Ezra 9–10	Acts 1
☐	15	Neh. 1–3	Acts 2:1–21
☐	16	Neh. 4–6	Acts 2:22–47
☐	17	Neh. 7–9	Acts 3
☐	18	Neh. 10–11	Acts 4:1–22
☐	19	Neh. 12–13	Acts 4:23–37
☐	20	Esther 1–2	Acts 5:1–21
☐	21	Esther 3–5	Acts 5:22–42
☐	22	Esther 6–8	Acts 6
☐	23	Esther 9–10	Acts 7:1–21
☐	24	Job 1–2	Acts 7:22–43
☐	25	Job 3–4	Acts 7:44–60
☐	26	Job 5–7	Acts 8:1–25
☐	27	Job 8–10	Acts 8:26–40
☐	28	Job 11–13	Acts 9:1–21
☐	29	Job 14–16	Acts 9:22–43
☐	30	Job 17–19	Acts 10:1–23

90-DAY BIBLE READING SCHEDULE

Day	Start	End	✔	Day	Start	End	✔
1	Genesis 1:1	Genesis 16:16	❑	46	Proverbs 7:1	Proverbs 20:21	❑
2	Genesis 17:1	Genesis 28:19	❑	47	Proverbs 20:22	Ecclesiastes 2:26	❑
3	Genesis 28:20	Genesis 40:11	❑	48	Ecclesiastes 3:1	Song 8:14	❑
4	Genesis 40:12	Genesis 50:26	❑	49	Isaiah 1:1	Isaiah 13:22	❑
5	Exodus 1:1	Exodus 15:18	❑	50	Isaiah 14:1	Isaiah 28:29	❑
6	Exodus 15:19	Exodus 28:43	❑	51	Isaiah 29:1	Isaiah 41:18	❑
7	Exodus 29:1	Exodus 40:38	❑	52	Isaiah 41:19	Isaiah 52:12	❑
8	Leviticus 1:1	Leviticus 14:32	❑	53	Isaiah 52:13	Isaiah 66:18	❑
9	Leviticus 14:33	Leviticus 26:26	❑	54	Isaiah 66:19	Jeremiah 10:13	❑
10	Leviticus 26:27	Numbers 8:14	❑	55	Jeremiah 10:14	Jeremiah 23:8	❑
11	Numbers 8:15	Numbers 21:7	❑	56	Jeremiah 23:9	Jeremiah 33:22	❑
12	Numbers 21:8	Numbers 32:19	❑	57	Jeremiah 33:23	Jeremiah 47:7	❑
13	Numbers 32:20	Deuteronomy 7:26	❑	58	Jeremiah 48:1	Lamentations 1:22	❑
14	Deuteronomy 8:1	Deuteronomy 23:11	❑	59	Lamentations 2:1	Ezekiel 12:20	❑
15	Deuteronomy 23:12	Deuteronomy 34:12	❑	60	Ezekiel 12:21	Ezekiel 23:39	❑
16	Joshua 1:1	Joshua 14:15	❑	61	Ezekiel 23:40	Ezekiel 35:15	❑
17	Joshua 15:1	Judges 3:27	❑	62	Ezekiel 36:1	Ezekiel 47:12	❑
18	Judges 3:28	Judges 15:12	❑	63	Ezekiel 47:13	Daniel 8:27	❑
19	Judges 15:13	1 Samuel 2:29	❑	64	Daniel 9:1	Hosea 13:6	❑
20	1 Samuel 2:30	1 Samuel 15:35	❑	65	Hosea 13:7	Amos 9:10	❑
21	1 Samuel 16:1	1 Samuel 28:19	❑	66	Amos 9:11	Nahum 3:19	❑
22	1 Samuel 28:20	2 Samuel 12:10	❑	67	Habakkuk 1:1	Zechariah 10:12	❑
23	2 Samuel 12:11	2 Samuel 22:18	❑	68	Zecharaih 11:1	Matthew 4:25	❑
24	2 Samuel 22:19	1 Kings 7:37	❑	69	Matthew 5:1	Matthew 15:39	❑
25	1 Kings 7:38	1 Kings 16:20	❑	70	Matthew 16:1	Matthew 26:56	❑
26	1 Kings 16:21	2 Kings 4:37	❑	71	Matthew 26:57	Mark 9:13	❑
27	2 Kings 4:38	2 Kings 15:26	❑	72	Mark 9:14	Luke 1:80	❑
28	2 Kings 15:27	2 Kings 25:30	❑	73	Luke 2:1	Luke 9:62	❑
29	1 Chronicles 1:1	1 Chronicles 9:44	❑	74	Luke 10:1	Luke 20:19	❑
30	1 Chronicles 10:1	1 Chronicles 23:32	❑	75	Luke 20:20	John 5:47	❑
31	1 Chronicles 24:1	2 Chronicles 7:10	❑	76	John 6:1	John 15:17	❑
32	2 Chronicles 7:11	2 Chronicles 23:15	❑	77	John 15:18	Acts 6:7	❑
33	2 Chronicles 23:16	2 Chronicles 35:15	❑	78	Acts 6:8	Acts 16:37	❑
34	2 Chronicles 35:16	Ezra 10:44	❑	79	Acts 16:38	Acts 28:16	❑
35	Nehemiah 1:1	Nehemiah 13:14	❑	80	Acts 28:17	Romans 14:23	❑
36	Nehemiah 13:15	Job 7:21	❑	81	Romans 15:1	1 Corinthians 14:40	❑
37	Job 8:1	Job 24:25	❑	82	1 Corinthians 15:1	Galatians 3:25	❑
38	Job 25:1	Job 41:34	❑	83	Galations 3:26	Colossians 4:18	❑
39	Job 42:1	Psalms 24:10	❑	84	1 Thessalonians 1:1	Philemon 25	❑
40	Psalms 25:1	Psalms 45:14	❑	85	Hebrews 1:1	James 3:12	❑
41	Psalms 45:15	Psalms 69:21	❑	86	James 3:13	3 John 14	❑
42	Psalms 69:22	Psalms 89:13	❑	87	Jude 1	Revelation 17:18	❑
43	Psalms 89:14	Psalms 108:13	❑	88	Revelation 18:1	Revelation 22:21	❑
44	Psalms 109:1	Psalms 134:3	❑	89	Grace Day	Grace Day	❑
45	Psalms 135:1	Proverbs 6:35	❑	90	Grace Day	Grace Day	❑

DAILY
DEVOTIONS

ABUNDANT GRACE

But after that the kindness and love of God our Saviour toward man appeared, Not by works of righteousness which we have done, but according to his mercy he saved us, by the washing of regeneration, and renewing of the Holy Ghost; Which he shed on us abundantly through Jesus Christ our Saviour; That being justified by his grace, we should be made heirs according to the hope of eternal life.—Titus 3:4–7

We live in a world in which much of life is dictated by scarcity and limits. There are only so many hours in a day, so much money in the bank, so many skills to apply to the task at hand; and as a result, there are often times when things we would like to see done cannot be accomplished. It is hard for us to comprehend the meaning of God's unlimited power, because nothing we know in this world is without limits.

Nowhere is that more clearly seen than in the matter of salvation. God provides freely what we could never obtain on our own. The sacrifice that Jesus made on the cross provides salvation through grace for all those who believe. No matter how many people accept Him as Savior, the saving grace of Jesus is never exhausted. No matter what sins a person may have committed, His grace is able to cover them all. Grace abounds more than sin ever could.

God's grace is not just extended to us at salvation, but it continues to be available for every part of life. "As every man hath received the gift, even so minister the same one to another, as good stewards of the manifold grace of God" (1 Peter 4:10). Grace is available to us for every challenge, trial, and temptation we face. There is no possibility of the supply being exhausted. There is no danger of going to God for help only to find that He is no longer willing to provide for us. We have overflowing abundant grace from God.

The Gospel in You Today

God's overflowing grace provides both salvation and victory for daily living.

MY SINS ARE GONE

Who is a God like unto thee, that pardoneth iniquity, and passeth by the transgression of the remnant of his heritage? he retaineth not his anger for ever, because he delighteth in mercy. He will turn again, he will have compassion upon us; he will subdue our iniquities; and thou wilt cast all their sins into the depths of the sea. Thou wilt perform the truth to Jacob, and the mercy to Abraham, which thou hast sworn unto our fathers from the days of old.
—**Micah 7:18–20**

The crew members of the British fishing boat *Galwad-Y-Mor* had no hint of trouble. The only unusual thing they noticed was extra tension on the line as they pulled in their crab traps, but they hoped that meant the traps were full. Instead, a huge explosion rocked the boat. As the boat sank due to the damage it had suffered, seven men were able to escape, although several suffered serious injuries. The Marine Accident Investigation Board determined that the explosion was the result of "old munitions on the seabed." The boat had accidentally caught an old mine, and it blew up as they pulled it toward the surface. The past had not stayed hidden beneath the sea.

That never happens with our sins. When God places them in the depths of the sea, they never resurface. There may be consequences and effects of sin that linger, but the sins themselves are buried where they will never be brought up against us again. When the devil accuses us, we have a Defense Attorney who has already paid the price for those sins. "My little children, these things write I unto you, that ye sin not. And if any man sin, we have an advocate with the Father, Jesus Christ the righteous" (1 John 2:1). His faithfulness ensures that our sins can never be placed back on our account or held against us again. They are in the sea for good.

The Gospel in You Today

Never let guilt or shame over past sins that you have confessed keep you from enjoying fellowship with God.

"TO WILL AND TO DO"

*Wherefore, my beloved, as ye have always obeyed, not as
in my presence only, but now much more in my absence,
work out your own salvation with fear and trembling. For
it is God which worketh in you both to will and to do of his
good pleasure.*—**Philippians 2:12–13**

Time and again, the Scriptures instruct us to
study, memorize, and meditate on the Word
of God and to be faithfully hearing it taught and
preached. We must obey those commands. But we
must also remember that the purpose of learning
the Bible is not primarily to *know* more, but to *obey*
more. Dr. George Truett said, "To know the will of
God is our greatest knowledge; to do the will of
God is our greatest challenge."

We see this principle in practice in the life of
Jesus. He was not content with merely knowing
what was right, but instead set an example of living
what was right. The writer of Hebrews describes
the motivation of Jesus this way: "Then said he, Lo,
I come to do thy will, O God. He taketh away the first,
that he may establish the second" (Hebrews 10:9).

When Jesus went to John the Baptist to be baptized, John realized that Jesus was God in the flesh and protested that he was not worthy to baptize the Lord. Yet Jesus insisted. "And Jesus answering said unto him, Suffer it to be so now: for thus it becometh us to fulfil all righteousness. Then he suffered him" (Matthew 3:15).

The temptation to think that we are growing in grace because we are growing in knowledge is very real. We only grow in grace, however, when we put into practice what we know. Reading every book available about lifting weights, running, or other exercise does nothing to improve our health. It is only when we actually do what we have learned that we benefit. The same is true in our Christian life. It is as we obey what the Lord is teaching us that we grow in grace.

The Gospel in You Today

Daily apply the truths of Scripture that you know to fulfill God's purpose for your life.

TIME AT THE FEET OF JESUS

And she had a sister called Mary, which also sat at Jesus' feet, and heard his word. But Martha was cumbered about much serving, and came to him, and said, Lord, dost thou not care that my sister hath left me to serve alone? bid her therefore that she help me. And Jesus answered and said unto her, Martha, Martha, thou art careful and troubled about many things: But one thing is needful: and Mary hath chosen that good part, which shall not be taken away from her.—**Luke 10:39–42**

There are many distractions that draw us away from God. Many of them are not wrong or evil in themselves. Some are good things that deserve our time and attention. The problem comes when we allow those good things to keep us from the most important thing. "And thou shalt love the Lord thy God with all thy heart, and with all thy soul, and with all thy mind, and with all thy strength: this is the first commandment" (Mark 12:30).

People are constantly looking for new methods and techniques to improve their spiritual lives, their finances, their families, and their sanctification. Yet, so often the answer is not in a new idea, but in practicing an old one—sit down at Jesus' feet.

Charles Spurgeon said, "I know this, that the death of all that is sinful in me is my soul's highest ambition, yes, and the death of all that is carnal and all that savors of the old Adam. Oh, that it would die. And where can it die but at the feet of Him who has the new life, and who by manifesting Himself in all His glory is to purge away our dross and sin?" The time that we spend with God is vital for our spiritual health and well-being. But it goes far beyond that. The time we spend with God is crucial to our growth in His grace. When was the last time you set aside everything else to get closer to Jesus?

The Gospel in You Today

No doubt there are many important tasks for you to accomplish today, but there is none more important than spending time with the Lord.

THE DANGER OF HYPOCRISY

Then spake Jesus to the multitude, and to his disciples, Saying, The scribes and the Pharisees sit in Moses' seat: All therefore whatsoever they bid you observe, that observe and do; but do not ye after their works: for they say, and do not. For they bind heavy burdens and grievous to be borne, and lay them on men's shoulders; but they themselves will not move them with one of their fingers.—**Matthew 23:1–4**

In one of their humorous true life story collections, *Reader's Digest* told about a lady named Callie Rough who was arrested in Middletown, Ohio, for shoplifting at a local Dollar General store. To make matters worse, she had two young children with her as she stole from the store. To top off the situation, among the things which she stole was a book titled 101 *Ways to Be a Great Mom*.

The religious leaders of Jesus' day made a great show of public righteousness. They offered loud public prayers, sounded trumpets to make sure people were paying attention when they gave, and spent a great deal of time telling other people how to live. The reason they hated Jesus so much was that He exposed their hypocrisy. They said the right things, but they did not live them.

Hypocrisy is bad enough in its own right, but it also makes us resistant to the call of God to repent. When we are living hypocritically, we can justify sin by pointing to good outward expressions while ignoring the evil in our hearts. When we think of ourselves as righteous, we see no need to change our ways. Jesus saw this in the Pharisees and revealed it: "And he spake this parable unto certain which trusted in themselves that they were righteous, and despised others" (Luke 18:9). They were content if people viewed them as doing right, without regard to whether they actually were doing right.

The Gospel in You Today

Yield to the Holy Spirit to bring true life change
in your heart rather than simply
acting the part outwardly.

UNLIMITED POWER

And what is the exceeding greatness of his power to us-ward who believe, according to the working of his mighty power, Which he wrought in Christ, when he raised him from the dead, and set him at his own right hand in the heavenly places, Far above all principality, and power, and might, and dominion, and every name that is named, not only in this world, but also in that which is to come:
—**Ephesians 1:19–21**

The power station with the most generating capacity on Earth is at the Three Gorges Dam on the Yangtze River in China. At full capacity, the thirty-two turbines that make up the power plant can produce over 22,000 megawatts of electricity. Each of these massive generators weighs more than 12,000,000 pounds. In 2015 the electricity production from Three Gorges was more than twenty times that of the Hoover Dam in America. In recent years, the power station has operated at less than full capacity because there simply isn't demand for the additional electricity that could be produced.

God's available supply of power is unlimited. In fact it is beyond our capacity to even imagine how vast it is. There is never any challenge, burden, or obstacle we face that would require God to exert Himself to solve. With mere words, God created the world. He does not need extra effort to solve our problems.

Yet as we serve the Lord, we all come to points when we find ourselves struggling to face the pressures in front of us or to experience His power through us. When we come to these times, we must remember that God is not limited in power; there is never a power failure with Him. We need to claim His promises and tap into the resources available to us. We are not helpless bystanders to the events around us. We are meant to be gospel witnesses, but we can only do that in God's power.

The Gospel in You Today

The same power that raised Christ from the dead is available to help you live victoriously today.

FAITH AND THE IMPOSSIBLE

By faith Abraham, when he was tried, offered up Isaac: and he that had received the promises offered up his only begotten son, Of whom it was said, That in Isaac shall thy seed be called: Accounting that God was able to raise him up, even from the dead; from whence also he received him in a figure.—**Hebrews 11:17–19**

When Abraham headed for Mount Moriah to offer Isaac as a sacrifice, as God had instructed, he could not know the outcome of his obedience. By human reasoning, if Abraham offered up Isaac, he would be coming back without his son—the very son God had promised decades before and had finally given after all hope seemed to have been lost. Yet now Abraham was preparing to obey God's command to kill his own son. Abraham's faith in God was so unshakable that he not only was willing to do that, but he also believed that after he did, God would resurrect Isaac. His faith is revealed in what he told the servants who accompanied him on the trip. "And Abraham said unto his young men, Abide ye here with the ass; and I and the lad will go yonder and worship, and come again to you" (Genesis 22:5). As far as we know, no one to this point in history had ever been brought back from the dead. Abraham simply knew that God had promised his descendants would come through Isaac, and he believed that what God had said was as certain as if it had already happened.

We, too, have the opportunity to walk in faith, believing God to do the impossible. When we trusted Christ as our Savior, He promised us eternal life. He also began a work of transformation in our hearts which He has promised to complete when we see Him. "Being confident of this very thing, that he which hath begun a good work in you will perform it until the day of Jesus Christ" (Philippians 1:6).

The Gospel in You Today

Trust God to continue His good work in your life.

REJOICING IN ADVANCE

Jesus answered, If I honour myself, my honour is nothing: it is my Father that honoureth me; of whom ye say, that he is your God: Yet ye have not known him; but I know him: and if I should say, I know him not, I shall be a liar like unto you: but I know him, and keep his saying. Your father Abraham rejoiced to see my day: and he saw it, and was glad.—**John 8:54–56**

When we talk about the faith of Abraham, we often think of a few specific ways he demonstrated trust in God: his willingness to leave his home for a new country, his long wait for a promised son, and then his obedience to God's command to offer Isaac as a sacrifice. The faith of Abraham is most clearly seen in the things he still believed even though he never saw them. "For he looked for a city which hath foundations, whose builder and maker is God" (Hebrews 11:10). The permanent nation of Israel did not become a reality until hundreds of years after Abraham's death. And the most important promise—Jesus—

did not come until thousands of years had passed. Yet Abraham rejoiced in God's promises, even those he did not personally experience.

There are hundreds of promises in the Word of God. Many of us have claimed those promises and found them to be true in our own lives. But the promises that we have not yet seen fulfilled are just as certain as the ones already completed. God has never failed to keep His promises, and we will not be disappointed in receiving all He has promised.

Because of the truth of the gospel, we can rejoice in advance to know that we have a sure home in Heaven and that we will one day see Jesus face to face as He promised: "And if I go and prepare a place for you, I will come again, and receive you unto myself; that where I am, there ye may be also" (John 14:3).

The Gospel in You Today

Rejoice today in the confidence that Christ is still fulfilling His promises in your life.

BEWARE OF PRIDE

And David said to Joab and to the rulers of the people, Go, number Israel from Beersheba even to Dan; and bring the number of them to me, that I may know it. And Joab answered, The LORD make his people an hundred times so many more as they be: but, my lord the king, are they not all my lord's servants? why then doth my lord require this thing? why will he be a cause of trespass to Israel? Nevertheless the king's word prevailed against Joab. Wherefore Joab departed, and went throughout all Israel, and came to Jerusalem.—**1 Chronicles 21:2–4**

David largely followed God during his time as king, and as a result he was blessed and Israel became more powerful. It appears that for a time, however, David became somewhat proud and self reliant, rather than depending on God as he had before, and that is why he decided to count the number of people in his kingdom. Despite receiving good advice against the plan, David insisted on having his way…and brought death and destruction on Israel as a result.

Although we are supposed to count our blessings, we should never make the mistake of counting on our blessings as our source of security or as if they are the result of our own doing. When we lift up ourselves in pride, we miss out on God's grace: "But he giveth more grace. Wherefore he saith, God resisteth the proud, but giveth grace unto the humble" (James 4:6).

We are utterly and completely dependent on God for every good thing in our lives. Whatever we have and accomplish is not to our credit, but to His. Jesus made our dependence on His power clear when He said, "I am the vine, ye are the branches: He that abideth in me, and I in him, the same bringeth forth much fruit: for without me ye can do nothing" (John 15:5).

The Gospel in You Today

Ask the Lord to search your heart for pride and to replace it with His grace.

WHAT THE HOLY SPIRIT DOES

And now, Lord, behold their threatenings: and grant unto thy servants, that with all boldness they may speak thy word, By stretching forth thine hand to heal; and that signs and wonders may be done by the name of thy holy child Jesus. And when they had prayed, the place was shaken where they were assembled together; and they were all filled with the Holy Ghost, and they spake the word of God with boldness.—**Acts 4:29–31**

Only a few weeks passed—fifty days—between the crucifixion and Pentecost. On that day, the disciples walked out onto the streets of the city where the Lord had been crucified, preaching that Jesus was the only way of salvation. These were the same men who had fled in terror when Jesus was arrested. These were the same men who Jesus found huddled in a locked room on Easter Sunday. This was the same Peter who three times denied knowing Jesus or being His follower.

Yet on Pentecost, everything was different. These men who had been terrified became bold witnesses of the gospel. Thousands were saved in those first few days of the early church. What made the difference? The disciples were transformed when the power of the Holy Spirit took control of their lives. They had not suddenly become more courageous in their own strength, but they were empowered by the Holy Spirit. "For God hath not given us the spirit of fear; but of power, and of love, and of a sound mind" (2 Timothy 1:7).

All of our efforts, abilities, methods, and programs will come to nothing if we work in our own strength. It is only in the power of the Holy Spirit that we become effective witnesses to the lost. As the old hymn puts it: "All is vain unless the Spirit of the Holy One comes down." The Holy Spirit plays many roles in the life of the believer, but one of the most vital is His empowering us to witness.

The Gospel in You Today

When you are fearful to witness, turn to God for His power and boldness.

WHY THEY STONED STEPHEN

And said, Behold, I see the heavens opened, and the Son of man standing on the right hand of God. Then they cried out with a loud voice, and stopped their ears, and ran upon him with one accord, And cast him out of the city, and stoned him: and the witnesses laid down their clothes at a young man's feet, whose name was Saul. And they stoned Stephen, calling upon God, and saying, Lord Jesus, receive my spirit.—**Acts 7:56–59**

Stephen started out by caring for the needs of widows in the church at Jerusalem, but he quickly also became a powerful and effective preacher. His preaching created such an uproar that the Sanhedrin brought him in to stand trial. Stephen preached the gospel of Christ with such power that his listeners literally put their fingers in their ears and screamed to make sure they wouldn't hear his voice.

What was the source of Stephen's powerful preaching? It was the very Word of God. Over and over, he cited the Old Testament Scriptures he knew.

Our thoughts, opinions, philosophies, and methods may have a place, but no human ability or plan can change the hearts of people. Only the Word of God has the strength to do that. "For the word of God is quick, and powerful, and sharper than any twoedged sword, piercing even to the dividing asunder of soul and spirit, and of the joints and marrow, and is a discerner of the thoughts and intents of the heart" (Hebrews 4:12).

The living Word of God proclaimed faithfully in the power of the Spirit of God will produce an effect. We may not see the result immediately, but we can be confident that when we declare God's Word, it impacts lives. "So then faith cometh by hearing, and hearing by the word of God" (Romans 10:17).

The Gospel in You Today

If you want to make a powerful impact on the world, be sure your ministry to others is filled with God's Word.

JESUS IS WORTHY

And I saw in the right hand of him that sat on the throne a book written within and on the backside, sealed with seven seals. And I saw a strong angel proclaiming with a loud voice, Who is worthy to open the book, and to loose the seals thereof? And no man in heaven, nor in earth, neither under the earth, was able to open the book, neither to look thereon.—**Revelation 5:1–3**

It took Stephen Mills thirty seconds to open the safe in the basement of the Vermillion Heritage Museum in the small Canadian town some 300 miles northeast of Calgary. The safe had belonged to the Brunswick Hotel, which closed in the 1970s. It was donated to the historical museum, but no one knew the combination. For forty years, various locksmiths and safe experts attempted to open it without success. Even the safe manufacturer was unable to provide a working combination.

Mills took his family on a visit to the museum in May of 2019. When the tour guide showed him the safe and shared the story, Mills looked at it for a few moments, and then tried a simple combination. He later said, "I gotta get down and try this for a laugh. I was doing it as a joke for the kids." Everyone was shocked when the safe opened. All those who had come before had failed, but Mills succeeded.

When the apostle John saw his vision of Heaven, he wept when he realized no one was worthy to open the seals. The angel told John that Jesus, having prevailed over death and the grave, was worthy. We have a precious loving Savior who is our friend and comfort. But we must never forget that He is also the King of Heaven, the omnipotent and almighty Lord. He gave Himself for us and is worthy of our worship and surrender. "And they sung a new song, saying, Thou art worthy to take the book, and to open the seals thereof: for thou wast slain, and hast redeemed us to God by thy blood" (Revelation 5:9).

The Gospel in You Today

Jesus is worthy of your praise and worship today.

THE BATTLE BELONGS TO GOD

And he said, Hearken ye, all Judah, and ye inhabitants of Jerusalem, and thou king Jehoshaphat, Thus saith the LORD unto you, Be not afraid nor dismayed by reason of this great multitude; for the battle is not yours, but God's. To morrow go ye down against them: behold, they come up by the cliff of Ziz; and ye shall find them at the end of the brook, before the wilderness of Jeruel. Ye shall not need to fight in this battle: set yourselves, stand ye still, and see the salvation of the LORD with you, O Judah and Jerusalem: fear not, nor be dismayed; to morrow go out against them: for the LORD will be with you.
—**2 Chronicles 20:15–17**

When three of the nation of Judah's neighbors allied together to fight against the Jewish people, there was no military hope for victory. Outnumbered by the enemy armies, King Jehoshaphat did the most important thing—he turned to God. God sent word through a prophet that He would not only give a victory, but that it would be a victory that did not require any effort on their part. As always, God did as He promised, and the Israelite army won without even engaging the battle.

This was not the normal way God gave victory to the Israelites. Most of their battles required them to fight. But this story reminds us that all of our battles—whether we must fight or whether God defeats our enemies—can only be won in God's power.

As Christians, we are in a spiritual battle and have been called to overcome the world, mortify the flesh, and resist the devil. We cannot do this in our own strength. We must instead obey the instructions of Ephesians 6:10–11: "Finally, my brethren, be strong in the Lord, and in the power of his might. Put on the whole armour of God, that ye may be able to stand against the wiles of the devil."

The Gospel in You Today

God has the power to give you victory in your spiritual battle today. Be strong in Him.

THE PURPOSE OF THE HOLY SPIRIT

Howbeit when he, the Spirit of truth, is come, he will guide you into all truth: for he shall not speak of himself; but whatsoever he shall hear, that shall he speak: and he will shew you things to come. He shall glorify me: for he shall receive of mine, and shall shew it unto you. All things that the Father hath are mine: therefore said I, that he shall take of mine, and shall shew it unto you.
—John 16:13–15

There is much confusion and false teaching today about the purpose and role of the Holy Spirit in the life of a Christian. But Jesus clearly laid out His purpose—to guide our lives in such a way that we will glorify Jesus. The Holy Spirit is not sent to indwell us so that we bring attention to ourselves, but so that we focus our attention on Jesus Christ. No self-promoting display of what is sometimes passed off as the power of the Holy Spirit is genuine. If the Holy Spirit is working, Jesus will be lifted up instead of us.

When we are filled with the Holy Spirit and walking in Him and being led by Him, what happens? Being filled with the Spirit does not mean that we are exempt from struggles with the devil. In fact, His power may place us in direct conflict with Satan. Indeed, this is exactly what happened in the life of Christ: "And Jesus being full of the Holy Ghost returned from Jordan, and was led by the Spirit into the wilderness" (Luke 4:1). It was not through *avoiding* Satan but through *defeating* him that the Spirit-filled Jesus was exalted. And how did Christ, filled with the Spirit, defeat Satan? He used the Word of God. Each time the devil tempted Jesus, He responded, "It is written…" and then quoted Scripture to counter Satan's temptation.

The Gospel in You Today

The Holy Spirit will always lead you to glorify Christ by overcoming temptation through the power of God's Word.

TRUSTING IN GOD'S PROMISES

Then spake the Lord to Paul in the night by a vision, Be not afraid, but speak, and hold not thy peace: For I am with thee, and no man shall set on thee to hurt thee: for I have much people in this city. And he continued there a year and six months, teaching the word of God among them. And when Gallio was the deputy of Achaia, the Jews made insurrection with one accord against Paul, and brought him to the judgment seat,—**Acts 18:9–12**

One of the great missionary leaders of the 1800s was Hudson Taylor. He first sailed from England as a missionary to China in 1853. Twelve years later, he sensed God was calling him to invite many more missionaries to serve in China with him. But he wrestled greatly over this decision because he was afraid of what would happen should he prove to be insufficient for the task. The conflict within only grew, until he came to a point of trust and surrender. Taylor described that moment: "On Sunday, June 25th, 1865, unable to bear the sight of a congregation of a thousand or more Christian people rejoicing in their own security, while millions were perishing for lack of knowledge, I wandered out on the sands alone, in great spiritual agony; and there the Lord conquered my unbelief, and I surrendered myself to God for this service. Need I say that peace at once flowed into my burdened heart?"

The promises of God are not given to us merely to admire, but to claim. We have a mission and assignment from Jesus to reach the entire world with the gospel. This is not a simple task, and we cannot in our own strength and power accomplish what God has set before us. But He does not intend that we should. It is in our faith to claim His promised power that we are able to face obstacles, challenges, and persecutions while remaining faithful to our task.

The Gospel in You Today

Trust God's promise to be with you as you witness for Him, and share the gospel with someone today.

HEALED SLIGHTLY

The wise men are ashamed, they are dismayed and taken: lo, they have rejected the word of the LORD; and what wisdom is in them? Therefore will I give their wives unto others, and their fields to them that shall inherit them: for every one from the least even unto the greatest is given to covetousness, from the prophet even unto the priest every one dealeth falsely. For they have healed the hurt of the daughter of my people slightly, saying, Peace, peace; when there is no peace.—**Jeremiah 8:9–11**

I magine if you sat across from an oncologist who was giving you the bad news that you had cancer. Immediately you would want to know what the prognosis was. Then you would want to know what the treatment plan would entail. How would you respond if that doctor said, "Well I think if you put a wrap on your wrist and a sling around your arm, that will take care of it"? You'd be looking for a new doctor immediately, because you would recognize the course of care he suggested would have no impact on your disease. This is what Jeremiah was referencing when he condemned the false prophets—they prescribed a cure that wouldn't work. The only "healing" they offered was a false assurance that brought temporary peace.

We live in a world that is diseased and broken by sin. We have the cure for the deadly problem of sin that works every time it is applied. "Come now, and let us reason together, saith the Lord: though your sins be as scarlet, they shall be as white as snow; though they be red like crimson, they shall be as wool" (Isaiah 1:18). Yet many times, like a child spitting out a medicine that tastes bad, people reject the cure for something that doesn't make them uncomfortable. Many churches, including some that are very large, offer kind words that people want to hear rather than diagnosing and effectively treating the problem. This may be popular, but it kills.

The Gospel in You Today

Share the truth of the gospel that provides the cure for sin with someone today.

WHAT GIVES GOD DELIGHT

And seek not ye what ye shall eat, or what ye shall drink, neither be ye of doubtful mind. For all these things do the nations of the world seek after: and your Father knoweth that ye have need of these things. But rather seek ye the kingdom of God; and all these things shall be added unto you. Fear not, little flock; for it is your Father's good pleasure to give you the kingdom.—**Luke 12:29–32**

Too many times people view God as if He were stingy, holding back on what He could do if He were willing. The Bible paints a very different picture. It shows God as a loving Father who cares for His children deeply. "For the LORD God is a sun and shield: the LORD will give grace and glory: no good thing will he withhold from them that walk uprightly" (Psalm 84:11). The reality is that God delights in giving to His children. He gives to us, not because we are deserving, but because it is His nature to do so.

The gospel itself is only possible because of God's gift of His Son. "For God so loved the world, that he gave his only begotten Son, that whosoever believeth in him should not perish, but have everlasting life" (John 3:16). Romans 8:32 emphasizes that such an amazing gift proves that God would never withhold what is good or needful for us: "He that spared not his own Son, but delivered him up for us all, how shall he not with him also freely give us all things?"

God is generous and giving by His nature. We do not have to convince Him to help us—He delights to do so. But when we neglect to pray for our needs, it is as if we think God is not willing to provide for us. We should instead pray for what we need and joyfully remember God's goodness to care for His children. When we ask God to provide, we are bringing Him great delight.

The Gospel in You Today

Pray today remembering that you have access to the divine resources God promises to His children and that He delights in meeting your needs.

THE FRUITFUL SEASON

Blessed is the man that walketh not in the counsel of the ungodly, nor standeth in the way of sinners, nor sitteth in the seat of the scornful. But his delight is in the law of the LORD; and in his law doth he meditate day and night. And he shall be like a tree planted by the rivers of water, that bringeth forth his fruit in his season; his leaf also shall not wither; and whatsoever he doeth shall prosper.
—Psalm 1:1–3

William Wilberforce probably did more than anyone else to end the slave trade in England and her colonies. Despite being right about the awfulness of slavery, Wilberforce found few allies in the fight. It took many years of effort and a willingness to keep going in the face of one defeat after another. One of the encouragements he turned to was a letter John Wesley wrote him not long before Wesley died.

Wesley said, "Unless the divine power has raised you up...I see not how you can go through your glorious enterprise in opposing that [slavery] which is the scandal of religion, of England, and of human nature. Unless God has raised you up for this very thing, you will be worn out by the opposition of men and devils. But if God be for you, who can be against you? Are all of them together stronger than God? Oh, be not weary of well-doing. Go on in the name of God, and in the power of His might." The Slavery Abolition Act gained the votes to pass three days before Wilberforce died.

God does not work on our timetable. He promises that anyone who delights in His Word will flourish, but even trees of righteousness only bear fruit in their season. There is a certain time of harvest, but it is only enjoyed by those who continue faithfully until they see the promises fulfilled. Do not be discouraged just because you have not yet seen that harvest.

The Gospel in You Today

Never give up your hope until you reach the season of harvest.

UNFAILING COMFORT

Yea, though I walk through the valley of the shadow of death, I will fear no evil: for thou art with me; thy rod and thy staff they comfort me. Thou preparest a table before me in the presence of mine enemies: thou anointest my head with oil; my cup runneth over. Surely goodness and mercy shall follow me all the days of my life: and I will dwell in the house of the LORD for ever.—**Psalm 23:4–6**

One of the realities of life is sorrow. All of us are confronted by loss, pain, disappointment, heartbreak, and despair. It is a wonderful blessing to have people around us to encourage, pray for, and support us during times of sorrow. But even if we have that human comfort, there is a far greater comfort available to us as children of God. And this source of comfort—the Holy Spirit Himself— never fails when we need it. Jesus promised His disciples, "And I will pray the Father, and he shall give you another Comforter, that he may abide with me for ever" (John 14:16).

There is never a day when we are alone or forsaken. There may be days when we feel that way,

THE GOSPEL IN YOU

but it is never reality. God is always with us. The Holy Spirit comes into our lives when we are saved, and He does not leave. He is the Comforter we can count on in distress.

God's comfort is based on His great love for us. Just as a shepherd would do whatever was necessary to care for his sheep, God will bring us help when we need it the most. The apostle Paul told the Corinthian Christians that our God is "the God of all comfort; Who comforteth us in all our tribulation" (2 Corinthians 1:3–4). Charles Spurgeon said, "He has loved thee long; He has loved thee well; He loved thee ever; and He still shall love thee. Surely He is the person to comfort thee, because He loves. Admit Him, then, to your heart, O Christian, that He may comfort you in your distress."

The Gospel in You Today

Because the Holy Spirit dwells in you, you can turn to Him for comfort and help today.

A SENSE OF URGENCY

Take heed therefore unto yourselves, and to all the flock, over the which the Holy Ghost hath made you overseers, to feed the church of God, which he hath purchased with his own blood. For I know this, that after my departing shall grievous wolves enter in among you, not sparing the flock. Also of your own selves shall men arise, speaking perverse things, to draw away disciples after them. Therefore watch, and remember, that by the space of three years I ceased not to warn every one night and day with tears.—Acts 20:28–31

Missionary Isaac Headland told of a poor Chinese woman who came to visit his wife. "Miss Kan, I'm so tired. I've walked fifteen miles today because I heard that you were going to the city soon, and I have not learned the Lord's Prayer yet." The missionary asked the exhausted woman holding a small child in her arms, "Why did you not wait till I came back again?" The woman replied, "Who knows whether I shall be living when you come again, I want to learn it now." Dr. Headland said the woman would not allow his wife to go to bed until the woman was able to recite the Lord's Prayer from beginning to end.

One of the tragedies of the church in our day is the casual way in which we approach spiritual things. When we read of Paul trying to reach people in Ephesus for Jesus both day and night while weeping, and doing it for three years, it seems strange to us instead of normal. The only day we know for sure we have available to work for God is *today*. Jesus said, "I must work the works of him that sent me, while it is day: the night cometh, when no man can work" (John 9:4). Rather than carelessly approaching life, we need an appreciation for the urgency of the work God has called us to do. In particular, sharing the gospel with others and helping new believers become grounded in the faith is of utmost importance.

The Gospel in You Today

Recognizing the importance of eternity, live today with a sense of urgency for what matters most.

THE IMPORTANCE OF MEDITATION

O how love I thy law! it is my meditation all the day. Thou through thy commandments hast made me wiser than mine enemies: for they are ever with me. I have more understanding than all my teachers: for thy testimonies are my meditation. I understand more than the ancients, because I keep thy precepts. I have refrained my feet from every evil way, that I might keep thy word.—**Psalm 119:97–101**

Every day we are bombarded with a vast array of information. It is easier than ever to stay connected to the world around us. Vast libraries are held in the small phones most of us carry everywhere we go. Media is intentionally created to cater to the shorter attention spans of the modern age. Sight and sound and information come at us in a flood. And in this flood, it is easy for us to lose sight of the vital importance of biblical meditation, which is taking the time to think deeply and meaningfully about the Word of God.

Dr. R. A. Torrey said, "A verse must be read often, and re-read and read again before the wondrous message of love and power that God has put in begins to appear. Words must be turned over and over in the mind before their full force and beauty takes possession of us. One must look a long time at the great masterpieces of art to appreciate their beauty and understand their meaning, and so one must look a long time at the great verses of the Bible to appreciate their beauty and understand their meaning."

The present controversies and issues of our world will fade into irrelevance. But the Bible endures forever. If we are going to walk as God commands, we must be people of the Word. Only through time spent thinking on God's Word can we grasp the full riches of His revelation to us.

The Gospel in You Today

As you spend time meditating on God's Word, your love for both God and His Word grows.

FINDING PURPOSE
IN LIFE

The Lord is my strength and song, and is become my
salvation. The voice of rejoicing and salvation is in the
tabernacles of the righteous: the right hand of the Lord
doeth valiantly. The right hand of the Lord is exalted:
the right hand of the Lord doeth valiantly. I shall
not die, but live, and declare the works of the Lord.
—Psalm 118:14–17

In May of 2019 the *Journal of the American*
Medical Association reported on a study that
has been going on since 1992. Beginning that year,
and each year since, the Health and Retirement
Study interviews adults in or near retirement age.
By following these people from year to year, and
by adding new participants to the study over
time, they are able to track the factors that have
the greatest impact on the lives and health of
thousands of people. They summarized their key
finding this way: "A growing body of literature
suggests that having a strong sense of purpose in

life leads to improvements in both physical and mental health and enhances overall quality of life."

What is true in retirement is true throughout life—those who have a definite purpose and goal in life tend to lead happier, healthier lives than those who do not. Every child of God is gifted differently, and there are many avenues through which we serve Him. But there is one thing that every living Christian can do—praise God. "I will sing unto the LORD as long as I live: I will sing praise to my God while I have my being" (Psalm 104:33).

When we recognize the importance of bringing glory to God, we understand that we always have an important purpose in our lives. We can always praise God. And who should praise Him more than those who have been redeemed by Christ? In the realist sense of the word, Jesus *is* our salvation.

The Gospel in You Today

Praise God today for His grace and the gift of your salvation.

NEWNESS OF LIFE

Therefore we are buried with him by baptism into death: that like as Christ was raised up from the dead by the glory of the Father, even so we also should walk in newness of life. For if we have been planted together in the likeness of his death, we shall be also in the likeness of his resurrection: Knowing this, that our old man is crucified with him, that the body of sin might be destroyed, that henceforth we should not serve sin.—**Romans 6:4–6**

When Paul wrote about the new life that comes after salvation, he was not speaking theoretically. His life story was a dramatic illustration of this truth. Paul went from being a leader of the persecution of Christians and attempting to stamp out Christianity in its infancy, to being one of the most powerful and effective voices of the gospel. Everything changed for Paul when he had his encounter with Jesus on the road to Damascus. From that day forward, nothing was ever the same for him again.

God saves us as we are, but He does not mean for us to stay that way. Peter wrote, "But grow in grace, and in the knowledge of our Lord and Saviour Jesus Christ. To him be glory both now and for ever. Amen" (2 Peter 3:18). The day will never come in this life when we have reached perfection. There is always more to learn about God and ongoing change needed in our transformation into the image of Christ.

The old life must be left behind if this is to take place. We cannot be looking over our shoulders and longing for the old things if we are to truly experience the new life. Christ didn't save us so we can keep living in our old sins; He saved us so we can put off our old sins and experience His life in us. "Therefore if any man be in Christ, he is a new creature: old things are passed away; behold, all things are become new" (2 Corinthians 5:17).

The Gospel in You Today

Rather than staying as we are, we are to look to Jesus and follow Him.

CHAMOMILE CHRISTIANS

And Saul was consenting unto his death. And at that time there was a great persecution against the church which was at Jerusalem; and they were all scattered abroad throughout the regions of Judaea and Samaria, except the apostles. And devout men carried Stephen to his burial, and made great lamentation over him. As for Saul, he made havock of the church, entering into every house, and haling men and women committed them to prison. Therefore they that were scattered abroad went every where preaching the word.—**Acts 8:1–4**

In ancient times, *Anthemis nobilis*—Roman chamomile—was widely used in medicines. The flowers were brewed into tea for treatment of digestive disorders, headaches, and to promote restful sleep. The Greeks also used Roman chamomile as a symbol for humility because, "the more it is trod, the more it spreads." Walking on the low-growing plants encourages the seeds to spread, and increases the crop.

THE GOSPEL IN YOU

When the church in Jerusalem was greatly persecuted, that did not end their gospel witness; it *increased* it. At a time when opposition to Christianity is becoming widespread in our society, it is good to remember that almost every book in the New Testament was written by someone who would eventually be martyred for his faith.

As our culture shifts from resistance to the gospel message to attempts to silence it, we must be conscious of the hand of God even in hardship and suffering. The mission we have been given to reach the world is not conditional based on the world being happy to receive the good news. Rather than feeling sorry for ourselves or silencing our voices when things get harder, it is simply another opportunity for us to spread the gospel.

The Gospel in You Today

Remember that God can use even difficulties and persecutions to give you an opportunity to witness for Christ today.

CHRIST LIVES IN ME

For if I build again the things which I destroyed, I make myself a transgressor. For I through the law am dead to the law, that I might live unto God. I am crucified with Christ: nevertheless I live; yet not I, but Christ liveth in me: and the life which I now live in the flesh I live by the faith of the Son of God, who loved me, and gave himself for me. I do not frustrate the grace of God: for if righteousness come by the law, then Christ is dead in vain.
—**Galatians 2:18–21**

People answer the question, "Who are you?" in many different ways. Some give a historical account of their family tree. Others cite their job, career, or hobby as an identifying mark. Some may share a philosophy or allegiance that helps define them. As children of God, all of us are called to identify with Jesus Christ, not just in a general sense, but in a specific way. We are to identify with His crucifixion. Without that identification, we cannot accomplish God's purpose for our lives.

The cross does not just represent the means of our salvation, but it also represents the means of our victorious new life in Christ. The Lord does not save us to leave us as we are, but to change us completely. Someone said, "There is a great difference between realizing, 'On that cross He was crucified for me,' and 'On that cross I am crucified with Him.' The one aspect brings us deliverance from sin's condemnation, the other from sin's power."

The process of transformation begins with our death to self. "And when he had called the people unto him with his disciples also, he said unto them, Whosoever will come after me, let him deny himself, and take up his cross, and follow me" (Mark 8:34). The apostle Paul said, "I die daily" (1 Corinthians 15:31). Only as we daily recognize our old nature as being crucified with Christ can we experience the reality of Christ living through us.

The Gospel in You Today

It is when we die to self, that we are able to experience the reality of Christ living through us.

THE REST OF THE HARVEST

But now is Christ risen from the dead, and become the firstfruits of them that slept. For since by man came death, by man came also the resurrection of the dead. For as in Adam all die, even so in Christ shall all be made alive. But every man in his own order: Christ the firstfruits; afterward they that are Christ's at his coming. Then cometh the end, when he shall have delivered up the kingdom to God, even the Father; when he shall have put down all rule and all authority and power.—**1 Corinthians 15:20–24**

Anyone who has ever planted a vegetable garden knows that it takes a long time for the produce to ripen and be ready to eat. You pick out a good spot and prepare the ground. You plant your seeds and water the soil. Eventually, a small plant emerges from the soil. You weed and water and fertilize and then weed some more. Day after day it seems like no measurable growth is happening. But finally, you get to eat the first tomato or cucumber or ear of corn. That's an exciting day, but it is just a small taste of what you are about to enjoy as the whole harvest comes in.

The wonderful things that we enjoy now as children of God are just "a foretaste of glory divine" as songwriter Fanny Crosby put it. The resurrection of Jesus Christ was not the end of God's plan; it was merely the first step of the final phase which will end with us experiencing eternal life and the world placed under His authority and rule. His resurrection was just the beginning of the harvest, for it awaits us as well. "Behold, I shew you a mystery; We shall not all sleep, but we shall all be changed, In a moment, in the twinkling of an eye, at the last trump: for the trumpet shall sound, and the dead shall be raised incorruptible, and we shall be changed" (1 Corinthians 15:51–52).

The Gospel in You Today

Christ already won the victory at the cross;
we are simply waiting for the rest of
the harvest to come in.

AN OPEN WAY TO GOD

And it was about the sixth hour, and there was a darkness over all the earth until the ninth hour. And the sun was darkened, and the veil of the temple was rent in the midst. And when Jesus had cried with a loud voice, he said, Father, into thy hands I commend my spirit: and having said thus, he gave up the ghost.—**Luke 23:44–46**

From the time shortly after the exodus from Egypt, God's presence on Earth was symbolized by the Ark of the Covenant. It was shrouded from view, first in the tabernacle and later in the temple in Jerusalem. Only one person, the high priest, was allowed in its presence, and that was just once a year on the Day of Atonement when he took the blood of the sacrifice to the Mercy Seat. There was a thick veil some thirty feet high that hid the Holy of Holies in the Temple.

But on the day Jesus died, that veil in the temple was ripped apart—not by human hands, but by a divine act of God. From top to bottom, the veil was torn, and the way to God was opened to us. Now, through Christ, we can enter directly into God's presence. "Having therefore, brethren, boldness to enter into the holiest by the blood of Jesus...which he hath consecrated for us, through the veil, that is to say, his flesh" (Hebrews 10:19–20).

We have an amazing privilege of access to God. The way has been opened once and for all. Yet too often we act as if there is still a barrier preventing us from coming into His presence. The reality of the torn veil does not benefit many Christians because they do not live as if it were true. We have daily needs, but instead of taking them to God in prayer, we try to work them out on our own. Prayer is not just for emergencies, and fellowship with God is not just for Sundays. There is a real and living God who has invited us to come before Him.

The Gospel in You Today

Although all Heaven and Earth bow before God, you get to call Him your Father.

THE REJECTED RULER

*And as they heard these things, he added and spake a
parable, because he was nigh to Jerusalem, and because
they thought that the kingdom of God should immediately
appear. He said therefore, A certain nobleman went
into a far country to receive for himself a kingdom, and
to return. And he called his ten servants, and delivered
them ten pounds, and said unto them, Occupy till I come.
But his citizens hated him, and sent a message after
him, saying, We will not have this man to reign over us.*
—Luke 19:11–14

God as the creator of everything is the only
rightful ruler of the entire universe. Yet
since before the world was created, there has
been rebellion against Him. Satan led an angelic
revolt meant to replace God on the throne. Adam
defied the only command he had been given to
do something in direct disobedience to God's
instruction. Israel rejected God for the false idols
worshiped by their neighbors. Jesus was rejected by
the religious leaders of His day because they feared
they would lose their privileged positions.

The world does not want God to rule over them. "The kings of the earth set themselves, and the rulers take counsel together, against the Lord, and against his anointed, saying, Let us break their bands asunder, and cast away their cords from us" (Psalm 2:2–3).

Although rebellion against God by the world is sinful, it is not shocking. But many Christians also struggle with the issue of obedience to God's commands. Often it is not that we do not know what we should do, but that we would rather go our own way. We do not have that right, because we do not belong to ourselves. "What? know ye not that your body is the temple of the Holy Ghost which is in you, which ye have of God, and ye are not your own?" (1 Corinthians 6:19).

The Gospel in You Today

The best way to affirm Christ's ownership of your life is to obey Him with glad surrender.

DESPISED BLESSINGS

And Jacob said, Sell me this day thy birthright. And Esau said, Behold, I am at the point to die: and what profit shall this birthright do to me? And Jacob said, Swear to me this day; and he sware unto him: and he sold his birthright unto Jacob. Then Jacob gave Esau bread and pottage of lentiles; and he did eat and drink, and rose up, and went his way: thus Esau despised his birthright.
—**Genesis 25:31–34**

In 1799 a twelve-year-old boy named Conrad Reed noticed a strange rock in the river where he was fishing near his family's home in North Carolina. He took the heavy rock home and showed it to his father. John Reed did not recognize what it was, and for the next three years, that rock was used as a doorstop in the family home. Finally it was showed to a jeweler who immediately identified it as a massive gold nugget—weighing seventeen pounds. The jeweler melted down the ore from the gold into a large bar and then bought it from John Reed for $3.50, which was only 1/1000 of its true value. Reed soon learned how much gold was really worth and established a profitable gold mine on the family farm.

God has given us so many blessings, yet far too often we do not value them as we should. Instead, we trade the valuable for fleeting trinkets and give up the eternal for the immediate. Like Esau, we magnify our needs and desires out of all proportion. Esau was in no real danger of dying from hunger after a day in the field, but he allowed his hunger to lead him to his foolish choice which had bitter lifelong consequences.

The Bible tells us that through the gospel we have "the unsearchable riches of Christ" (Ephesians 3:8). But sometimes, we treat these gospel blessings like the doorstop in the Reed home. Rather than recognizing their worth, we ignore them and live as if they don't even exist.

The Gospel in You Today

Gratitude for all that God has given us in Christ is a powerful protection against temptation.

THE KEY TO CLEANSING

But the other answering rebuked him, saying, Dost not thou fear God, seeing thou art in the same condemnation? And we indeed justly; for we receive the due reward of our deeds: but this man hath done nothing amiss. And he said unto Jesus, Lord, remember me when thou comest into thy kingdom. And Jesus said unto him, Verily I say unto thee, To day shalt thou be with me in paradise.
—Luke 23:40–43

The two men crucified with Jesus had earned their punishment by their evil deeds, but Jesus died as an innocent sacrifice for the sins of the world. As the crowd mocked Jesus on the cross, one of the thieves joined in. But the other responded with an acknowledgment of the perfection of Jesus and His rightful role as Lord of all. This thief was forgiven. Why? Because he put his faith in Christ. But to do that, he had to first accept responsibility for what he had done.

Until we come to the point where we are willing to acknowledge that we are wrong, we cannot experience the joy of God's forgiveness. The pattern stretches all the way back to the Garden of Eden where Adam blamed Eve and Eve blamed the serpent. It has continued throughout history.

The only way to forgiveness from sin is through the blood of Christ. And after we are saved, the key to walking in the joy of that forgiveness is confession when we have sinned. "If we confess our sins, he is faithful and just to forgive us our sins, and to cleanse us from all unrighteousness" (1 John 1:9).

Confession does not just mean to admit something. It carries the idea that we call sin the same thing God does—that we agree with Him that what we have done is wrong and accept personal responsibility for that sin. And when we do, we experience the joy of the cleansing only God can give.

The Gospel in You Today

Rather than trying to justify, shift blame, or excuse your sin, confess it and receive the joy of cleansing.

WHAT IT MEANS TO BE GODLY

Wherefore gird up the loins of your mind, be sober, and hope to the end for the grace that is to be brought unto you at the revelation of Jesus Christ; As obedient children, not fashioning yourselves according to the former lusts in your ignorance: But as he which hath called you is holy, so be ye holy in all manner of conversation; Because it is written, Be ye holy; for I am holy.—1 **Peter 1:13–16**

When people talk about godliness, there is often a great deal of confusion about what it means. Some equate godliness with a solemn form of religious observance. Others measure godliness by conformity to an outward code of behavior. While genuine worship and righteous living are important, godliness simply means that we are living as God says. The trait which He has chosen to emphasize above all others is holiness. In his vision of Heaven, Isaiah saw specially created six-winged seraphs whose sole responsibility is to continually proclaim God's holiness. "And one cried unto another, and said, Holy, holy, holy, is the

THE GOSPEL IN YOU

LORD of hosts: the whole earth is full of his glory" (Isaiah 6:3).

Peter wrote that we are to be holy "in all manner of conversation." In other words, in every part of our lives we are supposed to be holy. There is no area of life—business, home, church, school, hobbies, entertainment or anything else—that should not be subject to God's control. He calls us to be obedient to His Word, and that is the foundation of holiness. When our hearts are in tune with Him as they should be, we will not find it burdensome to give up the things of the world. God has nothing to do with the things of the world, and we shouldn't either. "And he said unto them, Ye are from beneath; I am from above: ye are of this world; I am not of this world" (John 8:23).

The Gospel in You Today

God develops the image of Christ in us
as we turn our lives over to Him in
daily choices of obedience.

LOOKING FORWARD

Not as though I had already attained, either were already perfect: but I follow after, if that I may apprehend that for which also I am apprehended of Christ Jesus. Brethren, I count not myself to have apprehended: but this one thing I do, forgetting those things which are behind, and reaching forth unto those things which are before, I press toward the mark for the prize of the high calling of God in Christ Jesus.—**Philippians 3:12–14**

The Christian life is meant to be lived with a forward focus rather than a backward one. While we should never lose our gratitude for what God has done for us in the past, that is not where He means for us to live. There are things ahead for each of us, no matter what stage of life we may be in, that God has planned for us to accomplish for His glory.

There is a future to anticipate even when we reach old age. "And it shall come to pass afterward, that I will pour out my spirit upon all flesh; and your sons and your daughters shall prophesy, your old men shall dream dreams, your young men shall see visions" (Joel 2:28). These dreams are not remembrances of the past but anticipation of the future. A. W. Tozer said, "I always get an uneasy feeling when I find myself with people who have nothing to discuss but the glories of the days that are past! Why are we not willing to believe what the Bible tells us? The Christian's great future is before him. Therefore, the whole direction of the Christian's look should be forward."

If we are always focused on the past—even if it is on past victories—we will miss reaching forward to the growth God has for us today and in the future. If you are still breathing, God still has a work to accomplish in and through your life. There is growth to be had in your walk with the Lord. There are lost people who need to hear the message of the gospel. Keep looking forward.

The Gospel in You Today

Today is a new opportunity to see victories won
for Christ by His strength in us.

FAMILY TRAITS

Jesus said unto them, If God were your Father, ye would love me: for I proceeded forth and came from God; neither came I of myself, but he sent me. Why do ye not understand my speech? even because ye cannot hear my word. Ye are of your father the devil, and the lusts of your father ye will do. He was a murderer from the beginning, and abode not in the truth, because there is no truth in him. When he speaketh a lie, he speaketh of his own: for he is a liar, and the father of it.—**John 8:42–44**

If you see a picture of three or four generations of a family together, you can usually identify common traits and characteristics. They may all be tall or all be short. They may all have the same hair or eye color. They may all look like the oldest person in the picture. The reason for that is one we all know well—they are related to each other. They have the same genetic heritage, and therefore they often look and act alike.

The same thing is true in the spiritual world. Despite what we often hear, man is not basically good. In fact the Bible tells us that the sin problem starts at birth: "The wicked are estranged from the womb: they go astray as soon as they be born, speaking lies" (Psalm 58:3). We got that sinful nature the same way we get our physical traits. They are passed down to us and we inherit them.

This is not a problem that can be addressed through our devotion, worship, giving, or good deeds. The only way we can get a new nature is to come to Jesus Christ and accept His offer of salvation by grace through faith. Only He can place us into the family of God, and He does this the moment that we receive Christ as our personal Savior. "But as many as received him, to them gave he power to become the sons of God, even to them that believe on his name" (John 1:12). From this point forward, God begins a transforming work to make us more like Christ (Romans 8:29).

The Gospel in You Today

God's goal for you is to conform you to the image of Christ, making you more like Himself.

RIGHT AFFECTIONS

If ye then be risen with Christ, seek those things which are above, where Christ sitteth on the right hand of God. Set your affection on things above, not on things on the earth. For ye are dead, and your life is hid with Christ in God. When Christ, who is our life, shall appear, then shall ye also appear with him in glory.—**Colossians 3:1–4**

The direction of our lives is determined by the things that we love. God calls us to love Him and that which is attached to Him rather than the things which attract those around us. "Love not the world, neither the things that are in the world. If any man love the world, the love of the Father is not in him" (1 John 2:15). It takes work and spiritual discipline to keep our affection set on the things of God in the face of distractions all around us.

Jonathan Edwards wrote, "Persons need not and ought not to set any bounds to their spiritual and gracious appetites, [instead they ought] to be endeavoring by all possible ways to inflame their desires and to obtain more spiritual pleasures. Our hungerings and thirstings after God and Jesus

Christ and after holiness cannot be too great for the value of these things, for they are things of infinite value. There is no such thing as excess in our taking of this spiritual food. There is no such virtue as temperance in spiritual feasting."

If we do not love God as we should, we will not walk in His ways for long. In Paul's final letter to Timothy, he lamented the condition of a man who had once been one of his stalwart helpers in the ministry: "For Demas hath forsaken me, having loved this present world, and is departed unto Thessalonica" (2 Timothy 4:10). We do not control the world around us, but we can control what we love. This is why God calls us to make an active choice to love Him above all: "Thou shalt love the Lord thy God with all thy heart, and with all thy soul, and with all thy mind" (Matthew 22:37).

The Gospel in You Today

It is impossible to love God and love the world at the same time—and we must love God.

WHO GETS THE CREDIT?

But Moses' hands were heavy; and they took a stone, and put it under him, and he sat thereon; and Aaron and Hur stayed up his hands, the one on the one side, and the other on the other side; and his hands were steady until the going down of the sun. And Joshua discomfited Amalek and his people with the edge of the sword. And the LORD said unto Moses, Write this for a memorial in a book, and rehearse it in the ears of Joshua: for I will utterly put out the remembrance of Amalek from under heaven.—**Exodus 17:12–14**

Joshua was tasked with leading the soldiers of Israel into battle against the Amalekites. But though the military conflict was real and intense, that is not where the real battle was taking place. Above the field of battle, Moses stood praying for victory. As long as he held the rod aloft Israel was winning, but when he grew tired, the Amalekites had the upper hand. The solution to Moses' fatigue was for Aaron and Hur to hold up Moses' arms until the victory was won. But after that victory, God had a pointed instruction to Moses for Joshua—to have this story written down and repeated in the future so that it would not be forgotten. God wanted His people to know that the real source of victory in that battle was the power of God.

The natural human tendency is for us to take credit for the things God has done—not just in physical victories, but in spiritual victories as well. It is only through the strength of the Lord that real victory comes. "Then he answered and spake unto me, saying, This is the word of the LORD unto Zerubbabel, saying, Not by might, nor by power, but by my spirit, saith the LORD of hosts" (Zechariah 4:6). Every work of grace in our hearts, every soul reached for Christ, every effectual moment of ministry is only by the strength of the Lord.

The Gospel in You Today

Depend on the Holy Spirit for spiritual victories, and then give Him the glory when they take place.

THE DEBT WE OWE

Now I would not have you ignorant, brethren, that oftentimes I purposed to come unto you, (but was let hitherto,) that I might have some fruit among you also, even as among other Gentiles. I am debtor both to the Greeks, and to the Barbarians; both to the wise, and to the unwise. So, as much as in me is, I am ready to preach the gospel to you that are at Rome also.—**Romans 1:13–15**

Most people are familiar with debt, having borrowed money for a house, a car, or an education. In these cases, we know who we agreed to pay back. They will send statements each month until the original loan has been repaid. If we do not make the payments, our lender will take steps to collect what we owe. While the Bible contains warnings about hastily borrowing money, it also tells us about another debt we owe—that of sharing the gospel with others.

Financial debts require an agreement. The borrower signs a note or declaration that the money is owed and that it will be repaid. Unlike those, the gospel debt comes to us not by a contract, but by a gift. Based on the gracious love of God for us and having become recipients of the incredible gift of salvation, we owe it to others to share the good news of the gospel with them as well. This is not the kind of debt where we pay someone back; it is the kind of debt where our plenty obligates us to share it with those who have nothing. To not share the gospel with the lost around us would be like eating a steak dinner in front of starving people. We simply owe it to others to tell them about Christ.

The response of others to the gospel is not our responsibility, but sharing the gospel with them is. Paul recognized that his debt extended even to those living in faraway nations. As Christians, we have what they need most, and the only hope they have for eternity. Our debt to them must be paid in full if we are to obey God.

The Gospel in You Today

We are God's plan for reaching the lost, and we must not fail to tell them how they can be saved.

THAT'S NOT ALL THERE IS

But the day of the Lord will come as a thief in the night; in the which the heavens shall pass away with a great noise, and the elements shall melt with fervent heat, the earth also and the works that are therein shall be burned up. Seeing then that all these things shall be dissolved, what manner of persons ought ye to be in all holy conversation and godliness, Looking for and hasting unto the coming of the day of God, wherein the heavens being on fire shall be dissolved, and the elements shall melt with fervent heat?—**2 Peter 3:10–12**

Mel Blanc had already been a successful voice talent for more than a decade when he took on the role of Bugs Bunny in the 1940 cartoon *A Wild Hare*. The new character made him one of the most famous people in America even though almost no one knew what he looked like. For more than sixty years Mel Blanc brought a variety of characters to life. At his request, his tombstone was inscribed with the catchphrase he popularized: "That's all folks."

In reality, however, death is not the end. The things of the world will one day be utterly destroyed. No fortune, inheritance, estate, or achievement will survive. But there are things that will last— the things which are eternal. Songwriter Al Smith wrote, "With eternity's values in view, Lord, with eternity's values in view; may I do each day's work for Jesus, with eternity's values in view."

The things to which we devote our lives are determined by the things which we value. There is a reason why the two great commands Jesus gave to summarize the entire law start not with our actions, but with our hearts (Mark 12:29–31). When we love the things of God, the eternal things, we will not easily be swayed by the temptations of the world. We will spend our precious moments on the eternal.

The Gospel in You Today

Rather than living today only for this life, live today with eternity's values in view.

WHO IS JESUS?

When Jesus came into the coasts of Caesarea Philippi, he asked his disciples, saying, Whom do men say that I the Son of man am? And they said, Some say that thou art John the Baptist: some, Elias; and others, Jeremias, or one of the prophets. He saith unto them, But whom say ye that I am? And Simon Peter answered and said, Thou art the Christ, the Son of the living God.—**Matthew 16:13–16**

The most important question each of us must answer is, "Who is Jesus?" And the obvious follow-up question is, "How will I respond to Him?" We often think of these questions in the context of salvation, and they are critical, for Jesus is the only hope of eternal life. But it is just as crucial for those of us who are saved to understand who Jesus really is and respond to Him properly if we are to walk in a way that is pleasing to God.

Jesus is not just a wonderful example, a great teacher, or a gentle friend. He is all of those things, but He is much more. He is God—the rightful ruler over everything. Jesus told His disciples, "Ye call me Master and Lord: and ye say well; for so I am" (John 13:13). Recognizing Jesus as Lord is not just calling Him that, but living as if we believe it to be true—living in obedience to Him. Jesus asked, "And why call ye me, Lord, Lord, and do not the things which I say?" (Luke 6:46).

It is wonderful and important to have the right doctrine, but unless that is matched by obedient living, our claims to be following the Lord are empty. He has the absolute right of both creation and ownership to call us to obedience. "What? know ye not that your body is the temple of the Holy Ghost which is in you, which ye have of God, and ye are not your own? For ye are bought with a price: therefore glorify God in your body, and in your spirit, which are God's" (1 Corinthians 6:19–20). We must not lose sight of the fact that Jesus is truly Lord of all.

The Gospel in You Today

Living in obedience to God's Word shows we understand and appreciate that Jesus is Lord.

Day

39

AN ONGOING CONFLICT

This I say then, Walk in the Spirit, and ye shall not fulfil the lust of the flesh. For the flesh lusteth against the Spirit, and the Spirit against the flesh: and these are contrary the one to the other: so that ye cannot do the things that ye would. But if ye be led of the Spirit, ye are not under the law.—**Galatians 5:16–18**

In 1337, disputes between England and France over succession to the throne and control of land broke out into open warfare. For the next 116 years, fighting continued in what came to be known as the Hundred Years' War. Though there were brief periods of truces and peace, the conflict, along with smaller wars between competing factions and allies of the two nations that went on at the same time, continued until France finally gained the upper hand and England renounced all claims to the French throne. Five generations of English kings ruled during the time the fighting lasted. It was a battle that must have seemed like it would never end.

THE GOSPEL IN YOU

As Christians we are part of an ongoing spiritual conflict that will never end until we reach Heaven. The new nature that we receive when we trust Christ as Savior competes with the old sinful nature that we inherited from Adam. The battle never ends. There are no days off or times when it is safe for us to set aside the weapons of spiritual warfare. Satan never gives up on his attempts to drag us down and destroy our lives. We must not grow weary of the battle and stop fighting, or we will surely be defeated. On the other hand, we can rejoice in the fact that, through the Holy Spirit, we are not powerless in this struggle. "For though we walk in the flesh, we do not war after the flesh: (For the weapons of our warfare are not carnal, but mighty through God to the pulling down of strong holds;)" (2 Corinthians 10:3–4).

The Gospel in You Today

Walk in the Spirit, and you will have access to God's mighty weapons to defeat sin and temptation.

AVOIDING DEFECTIONS

Take heed therefore unto yourselves, and to all the flock, over the which the Holy Ghost hath made you overseers, to feed the church of God, which he hath purchased with his own blood. For I know this, that after my departing shall grievous wolves enter in among you, not sparing the flock. Also of your own selves shall men arise, speaking perverse things, to draw away disciples after them. Therefore watch, and remember, that by the space of three years I ceased not to warn every one night and day with tears.—**Acts 20:28–31**

When Paul met with the elders of the church at Ephesus for the last time, it was a bittersweet moment. He had planted this church through preaching the gospel in Ephesus and then had poured years of his life into these people. The church had become one of the most important and influential churches in the world. But as strong as it was, Paul knew the church would come under attack, both from without and from within.

It is no different in our day. The truth is still under attack—not just from the world around us, but also from people inside of churches who spread false doctrine. There are some churches today where many people go because they like what they hear, but what they are hearing is far from the truth. There is always a temptation to make the message more accepted by removing the "rough edges." But that path leads to destruction.

Paul warned the Ephesians to be on guard for attacks against the truth. Maintaining a belief in the truth requires diligence, attention, and effort. No one remains in the truth accidentally. We must take heed to ourselves and purposefully stay rooted and grounded in God's Word and with God's people.

The Gospel in You Today

Remain alert to attacks against the truth—no matter their point of origin.

A HOLY TEMPLE

Flee fornication. Every sin that a man doeth is without the body; but he that committeth fornication sinneth against his own body. What? know ye not that your body is the temple of the Holy Ghost which is in you, which ye have of God, and ye are not your own? For ye are bought with a price: therefore glorify God in your body, and in your spirit, which are God's.—**1 Corinthians 6:18–20**

When Solomon set out to fulfill David's dream of having a permanent building for the Ark of the Covenant, to replace the tent in which it had been kept since the time of Moses, he left nothing to chance. Every detail was planned and prepared. The stone blocks for the walls and the wood beams for the roof were precut to fit, "So that there was neither hammer nor axe nor any tool of iron heard in the house, while it was in building" (1 Kings 6:7).

The Temple was dedicated with massive sacrifices and thousands of singers praising the Lord. The reason they took such extraordinary steps was that they realized exactly what they were building—a holy Temple for the living God.

As Solomon prayed to dedicate the Temple, he requested, "That thine eyes may be open toward this house night and day, even toward the place of which thou hast said, My name shall be there: that thou mayest hearken unto the prayer which thy servant shall make toward this place" (1 Kings 8:29).

There has not been a Temple in Jerusalem since the Romans destroyed it in 70 AD. But there is still a temple of God on Earth in each of His children, and we must not forget who we are. "Know ye not that ye are the temple of God, and that the Spirit of God dwelleth in you?" (1 Corinthians 3:16). And just as Solomon built that Temple to be solely for the worship of God, our temples must be kept holy as well. "If any man defile the temple of God, him shall God destroy; for the temple of God is holy, which temple ye are" (1 Corinthians 3:17).

The Gospel in You Today

Never forget how seriously God takes our personal commitment to holiness.

ONLY JESUS

*Then the priest of Jupiter, which was before their city, brought oxen and garlands unto the gates, and would have done sacrifice with the people. Which when the apostles, Barnabas and Paul, heard of, they rent their clothes, and ran in among the people, crying out, And saying, Sirs, why do ye these things? We also are men of like passions with you, and preach unto you that ye should turn from these vanities unto the living God, which made heaven, and earth, and the sea, and all things that are therein:—*Acts 14:13–15

When Paul arrived at the city of Lystra, he healed a man who had been crippled all of his life. When the people saw it, they were amazed. They treated Paul and Barnabas like gods, and were going to make sacrifices to them. It took everything Paul and Barnabas could do to stop the people from worshipping them and to point them to Jesus instead. "And with these sayings scarce restrained they the people, that they had not done sacrifice unto them" (Acts 14:18).

The noted English author Charles Lamb was once discussing with a group of other writers which historical figures they would most like to meet. Each named someone, most of them writers, and talked about how they would respond and what they might say. Finally Lamb said, "If William Shakespeare were to walk in, we would rise to meet him, but if Jesus came, we would fall to the ground to kiss the hem of His garment."

The world tells us to lift ourselves up and make sure everyone knows how good we are. God tells us to lift up Jesus Christ and make sure everyone knows of His offer of salvation. Any goodness or growth in our lives is the result of God's grace in us. When others see God at work in our lives, we have the opportunity to point them to Christ.

The Gospel in You Today

When someone praises you for what God has done through you, redirect the praise to Jesus.

FREE FROM THE GRAVE CLOTHES

Then they took away the stone from the place where the dead was laid. And Jesus lifted up his eyes, and said, Father, I thank thee that thou hast heard me. And I knew that thou hearest me always: but because of the people which stand by I said it, that they may believe that thou hast sent me. And when he thus had spoken, he cried with a loud voice, Lazarus, come forth. And he that was dead came forth, bound hand and foot with graveclothes: and his face was bound about with a napkin. Jesus saith unto them, Loose him, and let him go.—**John 11:41–44**

When news came to Jesus that His friend Lazarus was sick, the Lord did not respond immediately. This was not by accident, but by design. Jesus knew exactly what was going to happen. When He arrived in Bethany with His disciples, Lazarus had been dead for four days. Mary and Martha were heartbroken, not understanding why Jesus had not come in time to heal their brother. Jesus insisted on being taken to the graveyard, and called Lazarus back to life. This is a wonderful picture of what happens to us when we are saved. We are dead in our sins, with no hope of saving ourselves until Jesus comes.

After Jesus raised Lazarus, however, he was still wrapped tightly in the traditional grave clothes used at that time. Strips of cloth would be wrapped around the body, with spices sprinkled between the layers. Lazarus was alive, but he was not free. Similarly, coming to Christ for salvation does not remove the bindings of habitual sin that we have accumulated. While we now have the power of God to say "no" to sin, we activate that power by acknowledging we have it and resisting temptation as it comes. "How shall we, that are dead to sin, live any longer therein?...Likewise reckon ye also yourselves to be dead indeed unto sin, but alive unto God through Jesus Christ our Lord" (Romans 6:2, 11).

The Gospel in You Today

Remember you are dead to sin and alive unto God.

SOLDIERS OF THE CROSS

Thou therefore, my son, be strong in the grace that is in Christ Jesus.... Thou therefore endure hardness, as a good soldier of Jesus Christ. No man that warreth entangleth himself with the affairs of this life; that he may please him who hath chosen him to be a soldier.
—2 Timothy 2:1, 3–4

Though we remember him best as a gifted hymn writer, Isaac Watts pastored a church in London for a number of years. Watts learned early on the cost of faithfulness to Jesus Christ. His father, also a pastor, was twice imprisoned for refusing to be part of the official Church of England because of ways that church operated which were contrary to the New Testament pattern. When Isaac was a baby, his mother carried him to the prison to visit his father. Yet even seeing that hardship and suffering did not deter the younger Watts from following Christ himself.

Isaac Watts recognized that there are difficulties in the Christian life and those who would deter us from following Christ. Rather than just giving up, we must choose to be good soldiers for Christ in this spiritual battle. Watts captured this truth well in the song "Am I a Soldier of the Cross?" The first verse asks,

Am I a soldier of the cross,
A follower of the Lamb?
And shall I fear to own His cause
Or blush to speak His name?

We have a real spiritual adversary in Satan, and we must be willing to stand as soldiers and fight. "Whom resist stedfast in the faith, knowing that the same afflictions are accomplished in your brethren that are in the world" (1 Peter 5:9)

The Gospel in You Today

Stand strong today in your spiritual battle, being willing to endure hardness as a good soldier.

GOD'S UNFAILING MERCY

Behold my hands and my feet, that it is I myself: handle me, and see; for a spirit hath not flesh and bones, as ye see me have. And when he had thus spoken, he shewed them his hands and his feet. And while they yet believed not for joy, and wondered, he said unto them, Have ye here any meat? And they gave him a piece of a broiled fish, and of an honeycomb. And he took it, and did eat before them.
—Luke 24:39–43

When Jesus appeared to the disciples on the evening of the resurrection, they had already been told multiple times that He was alive again. Jesus had told them before He was crucified that He would rise from the grave. Mary and the other women who had gone to the tomb early that morning had told them that it was empty and that the angels witnessed that Jesus was alive. Peter and John had been there themselves and confirmed that the body of Jesus was gone. Then the two disciples who had been going to Emmaus and met Jesus on the road came back with the news that they had seen Him. Yet when Jesus appeared in their presence, they did not really believe it was Him. They thought they were seeing a spirit or a ghost.

Jesus, however, patiently explained to them that He was indeed alive. To confirm what they were struggling to believe, He ate food with them, something a ghost could not have done. This is a wonderful demonstration of God's mercy to us.

Despite the fact that we fail the Lord often and sometimes struggle to believe the promises He is fulfilling before our eyes, He still loves us. "Like as a father pitieth his children, so the LORD pitieth them that fear him. For he knoweth our frame; he remembereth that we are dust" (Psalm 103:13–14). God knows all about our frailty, so He strengthens us again and again, giving us reminders of His faithfulness.

The Gospel in You Today

God knows you better than anyone else,
yet He loves you unfailingly.

"THY WILL BE DONE"

He went away again the second time, and prayed, saying, O my Father, if this cup may not pass away from me, except I drink it, thy will be done. And he came and found them asleep again: for their eyes were heavy. And he left them, and went away again, and prayed the third time, saying the same words.—**Matthew 26:42–44**

Though Jesus was constantly teaching His disciples, there is only one thing recorded in Scripture that they specifically asked Him to teach them—to pray. In response, Jesus gave them what is commonly called the Lord's Prayer, although it would be more accurate to call it a model prayer instead. That well-known prayer begins with these words: "And he said unto them, When ye pray, say, Our Father which art in heaven, Hallowed be thy name. Thy kingdom come. Thy will be done, as in heaven, so in earth" (Luke 11:2).

Jesus was not teaching them something in the abstract. He was not giving them theories or ideas. He was telling them—and us—what matters when we pray. As Jesus modeled in this prayer and in His own prayer just before Calvary, every prayer must be offered in accordance with the will of God. There are times when we greatly desire a particular outcome to a situation. Yet even in those moments we must not insist on having things our way if God has something else planned for us. Thus in the Garden of Gethsemane, Jesus prayed, knowing the physical agony and spiritual torment that awaited Him, yet still praying in perfect submission to the will of the Father.

Prayer is not a means for us to get only answers that we will like. There are times, like Paul experienced when he prayed for the thorn in his flesh to be removed (2 Corinthians 12:9–10), that God uses hard things for His purpose. Even in the most difficult moments, we must pray for God's will rather than our own.

The Gospel in You Today

Pray for God's will to be done, knowing
you can trust your heavenly Father.

THE WORK OF UNITY

I therefore, the prisoner of the Lord, beseech you that ye walk worthy of the vocation wherewith ye are called, With all lowliness and meekness, with longsuffering, forbearing one another in love; Endeavouring to keep the unity of the Spirit in the bond of peace.—**Ephesians 4:1–3**

One of the most often mentioned characteristics of the first church in Jerusalem is that the people were in harmony and agreement. More than once we read that they were of "one accord." They gathered together day after day, eating, fellowshipping, worshiping, and praying. And their unity prepared them to make a great impact on their city. "And when they had prayed, the place was shaken where they were assembled together; and they were all filled with the Holy Ghost, and they spake the word of God with boldness" (Acts 4:31).

While it would be nice if unity and peace came naturally to us, both in our homes and in our churches, the reality is that it takes work. Unity is never accidental. It is the byproduct of God's people joining together in the fullness of His Holy Spirit and doing the work that is necessary to keep peace. As long as there are people involved, there will be hurt feelings, unkind words, disappointments, and divisions. But we do not have to allow these things to break our unity. Instead we can choose to work through the problems, addressing them rather than sweeping them under the rug.

Of course this is not easy. That is why Paul used the word *endeavouring*—it takes diligent, focused, intense effort. The Lord knows that such effort will be required, and through the Holy Spirit He gives us the power to put aside our focus on our own interests and consider instead the needs of others and the importance of unity. As Christians, we are united by the Holy Spirit that lives within us, but we must choose to put forth the effort to enjoy that unity with one another.

The Gospel in You Today

To experience the blessings of Christian unity, you must put in work to maintain it.

WAITING ON GOD

And, being assembled together with them, commanded them that they should not depart from Jerusalem, but wait for the promise of the Father, which, saith he, ye have heard of me. For John truly baptized with water; but ye shall be baptized with the Holy Ghost not many days hence.—**Acts 1:4–5**

In His last meeting with the disciples before returning to Heaven, Jesus gave them a final series of instructions to follow. The first step was one that many of us still struggle with today: to return to Jerusalem and wait. Soon the Holy Spirit would come on them and give power for effective ministry, but until then, there was nothing they could do.

Unless we are empowered by God, all of our labor and effort will be in vain. Yet for many people, waiting on God poses a real challenge. To overcome that challenge, we need to understand that God's timing is more important than ours and that He does not regard our time waiting on Him to be wasted.

Of course waiting on God must not become an excuse for laziness, but it is a vital part of our Christian walk. G. Campbell Morgan said, "Waiting for God is not laziness. Waiting for God is not going to sleep. Waiting for God is not the abandonment of effort. Waiting for God means, first, activity under command; second, readiness for any new command that may come; third, the ability to do nothing until the command is given." When John Milton went blind, it was a devastating blow to the gifted writer. But as he reflected on his new condition, he realized that God knew all about his circumstances. Milton wrote, "God doth not need either man's work or his own gifts…They also serve who only stand and wait." God is never in a hurry and never late. We must bend our schedules and timetables to His if we are to serve Him well.

The Gospel in You Today

Always be quick to obey God's voice,
but always be willing to wait on His timing.

ALPHABETIZING YOUR LIFE

Woe unto you, scribes and Pharisees, hypocrites! for ye pay tithe of mint and anise and cummin, and have omitted the weightier matters of the law, judgment, mercy, and faith: these ought ye to have done, and not to leave the other undone. Ye blind guides, which strain at a gnat, and swallow a camel. Woe unto you, scribes and Pharisees, hypocrites! for ye make clean the outside of the cup and of the platter, but within they are full of extortion and excess.—**Matthew 23:23–25**

It is very easy for us to allow our lives to be filled with things—often good things—that crowd out things that are even more important. Doing something that is good is no substitute for doing what matters most. Thirty years ago, *Readers' Digest* ran this story: "Michael Swenson was clocking late nights at the office working as a financial analyst for a large corporation. One night he got in around 12:30 and crawled into bed. His wife woke up and stated, 'You've got to alphabetize.' Swenson was

THE GOSPEL IN YOU

confused so he asked, 'What do you mean?' She replied, '*Wife* comes before *work*.'"

In every area of life, it is crucial for us to keep our focus on what comes first. The urgent will easily crowd out the important if we let it, leaving us with no time or energy to do critical things. When it comes to our days, we must set our priorities in the right order, or we will not be able to accomplish what God has set before us to do. And before anything else, we must put God at the top of our list. Nothing can be allowed to take His rightful place—the first place. Paul wrote, "And he is the head of the body, the church: who is the beginning, the firstborn from the dead; that in all things he might have the preeminence" (Colossians 1:18). There is no part of life where God should not come first.

The Gospel in You Today

Give Christ priority over
everything else in your life.

STAY ON GUARD

Be sober, be vigilant; because your adversary the devil, as a roaring lion, walketh about, seeking whom he may devour: Whom resist stedfast in the faith, knowing that the same afflictions are accomplished in your brethren that are in the world. But the God of all grace, who hath called us unto his eternal glory by Christ Jesus, after that ye have suffered a while, make you perfect, stablish, strengthen, settle you.—**1 Peter 5:8–10**

In February of 2014, an Ethiopian Airlines 767 was hijacked by the co-pilot. His plan was to fly to Switzerland and request asylum there. Once it became known that the plane was no longer on its original flight plan, Italian Air Force jets responded and followed it as it made its way north. At the border, French Air Force planes took over the escort task. But when the hijacked plane crossed into Swiss airspace, the French planes had to stay with it. It turned out that due to budget cuts and noise regulations, Swiss Air Force planes were only operating during daytime business hours—leaving the nation undefended and forced to rely on others for protection.

Twenty-four hours a day, seven days a week, we have an enemy who is active and committed to our destruction. He doesn't work only during business hours. He doesn't take days off. We must be constantly and continually on guard so that we are not taken by surprise. Jesus warned Peter that Satan was after him in a special way, but when He returned, Jesus found Peter sleeping instead of praying. He warned, "Watch and pray, that ye enter not into temptation: the spirit indeed is willing, but the flesh is weak" (Matthew 26:41).

The devil is looking for opportunities to take us down. If you were strong against temptation yesterday, he will still come back today. Through the power of God, it is possible for us to have victory over sin and the devil, but it requires us to be alert and vigilant to resist his temptations.

The Gospel in You Today

Victorious Christian living requires constant guarding against the temptations of the devil.

BEARING FRUIT

Henceforth I call you not servants; for the servant knoweth not what his lord doeth: but I have called you friends; for all things that I have heard of my Father I have made known unto you. Ye have not chosen me, but I have chosen you, and ordained you, that ye should go and bring forth fruit, and that your fruit should remain: that whatsoever ye shall ask of the Father in my name, he may give it you.—**John 15:15–16**

When John Endicott arrived in the New World to serve as governor of the Massachusetts Bay Colony, he wanted to do things that would encourage more people to make the trip from England. Realizing that one of the things they would most miss would be fruit trees, he arranged for a number of varieties to be imported. Sometime in the early 1630s, Endicott planted a pear tree near Salem, Massachusetts. On that day he told the family and friends who were there, "No doubt when we have gone the tree will still be alive." In fact, almost four hundred years later, the Endicott Pear Tree is still alive and still bearing fruit.

God intends for His children to be fruitful, not just for a brief time, but for all of our lives. He wants us to be consistently bringing forth fruit, season after season and year after year. "And he shall be like a tree planted by the rivers of water, that bringeth forth his fruit in his season; his leaf also shall not wither; and whatsoever he doeth shall prosper" (Psalm 1:3). The impact of a fruitful tree is not fully felt in a few years or even in a decade, but over many years—and sometimes over multiple generations. There is much that we do from day to day that will quickly fade. But if we are deeply connected to the Lord, our lives will also produce fruit that will be a continuing testimony to His grace and power. "And let us not be weary in well doing: for in due season we shall reap, if we faint not" (Galatians 6:9).

The Gospel in You Today

A Christian who is abiding in Christ day by day will, over time, produce fruit to the glory of God.

GOD'S GLORIOUS GRACE

To the praise of the glory of his grace, wherein he hath made us accepted in the beloved.—**Ephesians 1:6**

The entry of sin into the world did not take God by surprise. There was only one prohibition He had given to Adam—not to eat from the tree of the knowledge of good and evil. Yet even with only one rule in place, obedience was more than Adam could manage, and he sinned. Since that day, every person born into the world has been born with a sinful nature. That sin alienates us from God, and despite His love for us, His justice and holiness demand that the price for sin be paid. The only hope we have for Heaven is to receive what we do not deserve through grace.

That is why Jesus came into the world. In love, He paid the price for our sins so that salvation could be offered. Just as Adam brought sin into the world and affected everyone who followed, Jesus brought grace into the world, which is for all who will believe. "But not as the offence, so also is the free gift. For if through the offence of one many be dead, much more the grace of God, and the gift by grace, which is by one man, Jesus Christ, hath abounded unto many" (Romans 5:15).

So many people are trying to earn their salvation. They hope that the things they do or avoid doing will somehow improve their standing with God. But our only hope is His grace. The best that we can do falls short of His perfect righteousness. Even some Christians are trying to earn God's acceptance. They live as if God is an angry Father holding them at arm's length until they prove they are worthy of His grace. The truth is that we will never be worthy, but we are fully and truly "accepted in the beloved."

The Gospel in You Today

Live today with the confidence that you are accepted in Christ because of His grace, and look for an opportunity to share the glorious message of grace with someone who doesn't know Christ.

AN UNFAILING GRIP

My sheep hear my voice, and I know them, and they follow me: And I give unto them eternal life; and they shall never perish, neither shall any man pluck them out of my hand. My Father, which gave them me, is greater than all; and no man is able to pluck them out of my Father's hand. I and my Father are one.—**John 10:27–30**

There are about twenty different contests held around the world each year to determine who has the strongest hands. One of the most common competitions is the "pinch grip" where a weight is held only between the fingers and the thumb, and is not allowed to touch the palm of the hand. In 2010 at the World of Grip championships, David Horne set a new world record, lifting more than 260 pounds with just his fingers. He then went on to win the championship in five of the next six years as well.

While David Horne's hands are certainly very strong, they are nothing compared to God's hands which hold His children safe and secure. Many Christians live with insecurity, doubt, and fear

THE GOSPEL IN YOU

when God wants them to live in perfect confidence. The idea that someone who has been saved can then somehow lose that salvation is contrary to what Jesus taught. Anyone who has genuinely trusted Christ as His Savior is as safe as if he were already in Heaven.

It is true that there are things we can do which will displease God and things we can do which will bring difficult consequences into our lives. We surely must not use the fact that we are secure in Christ to indulge in sin. "What shall we say then? Shall we continue in sin, that grace may abound? God forbid. How shall we, that are dead to sin, live any longer therein?" (Romans 6:1–2). But when we sin, God does not turn His back on us. He does not take away the free gift of salvation that He has given to us.

The Gospel in You Today

Rejoice in the security of God's promise that once you belong to Him, you are His forever.

WHO'S IN CHARGE?

But ye are not in the flesh, but in the Spirit, if so be that the Spirit of God dwell in you. Now if any man have not the Spirit of Christ, he is none of his. And if Christ be in you, the body is dead because of sin; but the Spirit is life because of righteousness. But if the Spirit of him that raised up Jesus from the dead dwell in you, he that raised up Christ from the dead shall also quicken your mortal bodies by his Spirit that dwelleth in you.
—**Romans 8:9–11**

Many years ago, a group of men became convinced of the need for a genuine revival in their city. They agreed to meet together to work on plans for bringing someone to town to preach. Soon several had suggested D. L. Moody be asked to come, as he had already held great meetings in both America and England and had seen great blessings on his work. The story goes that one man rose to object. "You speak as if D. L. Moody had a monopoly on God," he declared. One of the men replied, "No, God has a monopoly on D. L. Moody."

It is true that every Christian has the same Holy Spirit. But it is also true that the Holy Spirit does not have the same level of control over every Christian. It is only as we yield control of our lives to Him that He will work in and through us as He is able to do. There is a constant and ongoing battle in our lives between the flesh and the Spirit. "For the flesh lusteth against the Spirit, and the Spirit against the flesh: and these are contrary the one to the other: so that ye cannot do the things that ye would" (Galatians 5:17). The power to live spiritually is available, but it cannot be applied if we are focused on fulfilling our own desires and interests. "This I say then, Walk in the Spirit, and ye shall not fulfil the lust of the flesh....If we live in the Spirit, let us also walk in the Spirit" (Galatians 5:16, 25).

The Gospel in You Today

It is impossible for you to walk in the Spirit and insist on your own way at the same time.

FORGIVEN AND SET FREE

And they which heard it, being convicted by their own conscience, went out one by one, beginning at the eldest, even unto the last: and Jesus was left alone, and the woman standing in the midst. When Jesus had lifted up himself, and saw none but the woman, he said unto her, Woman, where are those thine accusers? hath no man condemned thee? She said, No man, Lord. And Jesus said unto her, Neither do I condemn thee: go, and sin no more.—**John 8:9–11**

In an attempt to trap Jesus, the religious leaders brought an adulterous woman before Him and asked what should be done. They thought they had placed Jesus in a no-win situation. If He said she should be stoned, they would accuse Him of breaking Roman law. If He said she should not be stoned, they would accuse Him of breaking Jewish law. Instead of falling into their trap, Jesus invited those who were without sin themselves to carry out the punishment they were suggesting He invoke. Jesus' answer was consistent with the law of

Moses which required those who testified against someone in a capital case to carry out the sentence themselves (Deuteronomy 17:7).

After the ashamed accusers (who were not really interested in following the law) had left, Jesus gave the woman two things that she desperately needed: forgiveness for past sins and the ability not to be bound by her past life.

When we trust Christ as our Savior, we are not just forgiven but also set free. Paul wrote, "Knowing this, that our old man is crucified with him, that the body of sin might be destroyed, that henceforth we should not serve sin. For he that is dead is freed from sin" (Romans 6:6–7). No believer is compelled to sin, but instead can walk in freedom. We now have no condemnation *and* the power to resist the sins of our past.

The Gospel in You Today

Walk victoriously in the power you have been given to reject the bondage of sin.

IT'S NOT HOPELESS

Who against hope believed in hope, that he might become the father of many nations, according to that which was spoken, So shall thy seed be. And being not weak in faith, he considered not his own body now dead, when he was about an hundred years old, neither yet the deadness of Sara's womb: He staggered not at the promise of God through unbelief; but was strong in faith, giving glory to God; And being fully persuaded that, what he had promised, he was able also to perform.
—**Romans 4:18–21**

Abraham waited some twenty-five years for the arrival of his promised son who would fulfill God's promise to raise up a great nation. During that time, he had no human reason to expect a son would ever come. In fact, it was physically impossible for Sarah to bear a child. Yet in that long season when there seemed to be no reason for hope, Abraham still believed. And he continued in faith until the promised child, Isaac, was finally born. Marshal Ferdinand Foch, who commanded the French army during much of World War I said,

"There are no hopeless situations: there are only men who have grown hopeless about them."

The reason we can have hope in what may seem to others to be hopeless situations is that our hope is not based on our ability, resources, knowledge, or strength. Our hope is in the Lord who faithfully keeps every promise He has made. This is why the psalmist could counsel himself to hope in the Lord: "Why art thou cast down, O my soul? and why art thou disquieted within me? hope thou in God: for I shall yet praise him, who is the health of my countenance, and my God" (Psalm 42:11). God is not only the source of the promises we have received, but He is also the guarantee that they will be fulfilled. "In hope of eternal life, which God, that cannot lie, promised before the world began" (Titus 1:2).

The Gospel in You Today

Put your hope in God today;
He not only *does* not lie, but He *cannot* lie.

"MEMBERS IN ONE BODY"

For I say, through the grace given unto me, to every man that is among you, not to think of himself more highly than he ought to think; but to think soberly, according as God hath dealt to every man the measure of faith. For as we have many members in one body, and all members have not the same office: So we, being many, are one body in Christ, and every one members one of another.
—**Romans 12:3–5**

In May of 1863, near Chancellorsville, Virginia, the Union Army outnumbered the Confederates under Robert E. Lee almost two to one. They were confident of victory, but a daring decision by Lee to split his forces changed that. Lee sent nearly half his outnumbered troops on a long march under the command of Thomas "Stonewall" Jackson to strike the Union forces from behind. The surprise attack worked, winning one of the biggest victories of the entire war. But it came at a high price.

When the fighting ended on the evening of May 2, Jackson and some of his aides rode out to scout the field of battle. When they returned, they were mistaken in the darkness for Union cavalry attempting a raid, and their own troops opened fire on them. Jackson was hit by three bullets. Doctors amputated his arm in an effort to save his life, but on May 10, Lee's best and most effective general died—killed by his own men.

Too often Christians forget that they are all members of one body. Churches are riven with dissension and discord, when they are meant to be sources of encouragement and strength. That help we give and receive is one of the primary reasons behind the command God gave us to be faithful in church attendance. "Not forsaking the assembling of ourselves together, as the manner of some is; but exhorting one another: and so much the more, as ye see the day approaching" (Hebrews 10:25).

The Gospel in You Today

Look for ways to support and encourage those in your church family.

THE MIRROR CAN'T CHANGE YOUR REFLECTION

But be ye doers of the word, and not hearers only, deceiving your own selves. For if any be a hearer of the word, and not a doer, he is like unto a man beholding his natural face in a glass: For he beholdeth himself, and goeth his way, and straightway forgetteth what manner of man he was. But whoso looketh into the perfect law of liberty, and continueth therein, he being not a forgetful hearer, but a doer of the work, this man shall be blessed in his deed.
—**James 1:22–25**

Most of us look at ourselves in the mirror on a regular basis. We have mirrors in our homes, our offices, and our cars. All of those mirrors show a reflection of what is in front of them. Sometimes we are pleased with what we see, and sometimes we realize that some kind of change needs to be made, but the mirror never makes those changes for us.

When James compared the Bible to a mirror, he noted that by looking into the Word of God, we see what needs to be changed in our lives. But just like a physical mirror, the Bible can't make those changes. We need to be obedient to *do* what God instructs. A Christian who only *hears* the Bible without *doing* anything with what he learns is like someone who looks in a mirror to see food on his face and walks away without doing anything about it.

The purpose of God for our lives is for us to become more and more like Jesus—that we would be "conformed to the image of his Son" (Romans 8:29). This transformation happens over time as we look into God's Word, remain sensitive to the conviction of His Spirit, and make the changes He instructs us to make.

The Gospel in You Today

Every time you open God's Word or hear it preached, ask yourself, "What does God want me to do with what I have just heard?"

LIVING IN FORGIVENESS

And Joseph said unto his brethren, I am Joseph; doth my father yet live? And his brethren could not answer him; for they were troubled at his presence. And Joseph said unto his brethren, Come near to me, I pray you. And they came near. And he said, I am Joseph your brother, whom ye sold into Egypt. Now therefore be not grieved, nor angry with yourselves, that ye sold me hither: for God did send me before you to preserve life.—**Genesis 45:3–5**

When Joseph's brothers sold him into slavery and made Jacob believe his favorite son had been killed by a wild animal, they committed a great evil. Yet when they were finally reunited with Joseph, though he had the power to inflict any punishment he wished on them, he forgave them. Joseph was willing to forgive because he recognized God had been at work. The problem was that his brothers had a hard time accepting that they had been forgiven.

Seventeen years passed before Jacob died. When they returned to Egypt after burying Jacob in the Promised Land, they feared that Joseph had just been biding his time. "And when Joseph's brethren saw that their father was dead, they said, Joseph will peradventure hate us, and will certainly requite us all the evil which we did unto him" (Genesis 50:15). They had been forgiven, but they were still living with guilt and shame for what they had done.

Sometimes we do that in relation to God's forgiveness. Jesus paid the debt for our sin on the cross, and when we trusted Him as our Savior, He fully and freely forgave us. Yes, we may experience consequences in our lives for past actions, but the guilt has been removed. "There is therefore now no condemnation to them which are in Christ Jesus, who walk not after the flesh, but after the Spirit" (Romans 8:1).

The Gospel in You Today

Do not allow the devil to convince you that you are guilty when Christ has already forgiven you.

THE SPIRIT OF ADOPTION

For ye have not received the spirit of bondage again to fear;
but ye have received the Spirit of adoption, whereby we
cry, Abba, Father. The Spirit itself beareth witness with
our spirit, that we are the children of God: And if children,
then heirs; heirs of God, and joint-heirs with Christ; if so
be that we suffer with him, that we may be also glorified
together.—**Romans 8:15–17**

In 44 BC Gaius Octavius Thurinus, just seventeen years of age, was named in the will of the assassinated Julius Caesar as his adopted heir. Caesar was his great uncle, and Octavius spent much of his youth with Caesar's sister. His courage and resourcefulness even as a teenager when he joined the army fighting in Spain led to Casear's decision. In 27 BC Octavius' name was officially changed to Caesar Augustus, and he became Rome's first emperor. During Caesar Augustus' forty-year reign, the empire doubled in size. Not long before his death he said, "I found Rome of clay; I leave it to you of marble." None of that would have happened had not Julius Caesar adopted him into his family and named Octavian heir to all he possessed.

Every person born into the world is born into the "wrong family." Because of the fall, each of us are born with a sin nature. The only hope that we have is for God's grace to place us into His family, and He freely offers this to all who trust in Christ.

When we become a child of God, we receive the Holy Spirit to guide us and give us confidence in our new standing and relationship. We did nothing to deserve or gain membership in God's family. But once we have been placed there by grace, we have a responsibility to live holy lives. "But fornication, and all uncleanness, or covetousness, let it not be once named among you, as becometh saints" (Ephesians 5:3).

The Gospel in You Today

Honor your heavenly Father by living in a way that is worthy of His name.

THE IMPORTANCE OF SANCTIFICATION

Nevertheless, brethren, I have written the more boldly unto you in some sort, as putting you in mind, because of the grace that is given to me of God, That I should be the minister of Jesus Christ to the Gentiles, ministering the gospel of God, that the offering up of the Gentiles might be acceptable, being sanctified by the Holy Ghost. I have therefore whereof I may glory through Jesus Christ in those things which pertain to God.—**Romans 15:15–17**

A brilliant Christian scholar, Henry Martyn, was headed toward a lucrative legal career when he heard a man named Charles Simeon tell about what William Carey was doing as a missionary in India. He immediately changed course and began training to go to India himself. Martyn set sail for India in 1805. He died just seven years later, at the age of thirty-one. But in that brief period of ministry, Martyn translated the New Testament into three different languages and had a powerful impact for the gospel on both India and Iran.

Although Martyn spent his life declaring the gospel to others, he did not neglect to see the results of the gospel in his own life. Of his walk with the Lord, he said, "Let me be taught that the first great business on Earth is the sanctification of my own soul."

The purpose of God for our lives is for us to be sanctified—to become more like the image of His perfect Son, Jesus Christ. This is not done through our determination, will power, or strength, but by the Holy Spirit as we yield our lives to His control. No matter how hard we try or how diligently we work, the process of sanctification is beyond human power to achieve. "Are ye so foolish? having begun in the Spirit, are ye now made perfect by the flesh?" (Galatians 3:3). But as we yield to Him, our lives bring honor and glory to God as He intends.

The Gospel in You Today

The result of the gospel in your life should be a daily transformation into the image of Christ.

THE WORTHY WALK

*For this cause we also, since the day we heard it, do not
cease to pray for you, and to desire that ye might be filled
with the knowledge of his will in all wisdom and spiritual
understanding; That ye might walk worthy of the Lord
unto all pleasing, being fruitful in every good work, and
increasing in the knowledge of God; Strengthened with all
might, according to his glorious power, unto all patience
and longsuffering with joyfulness;*—**Colossians 1:9–11**

The idea that people are basically good and will
usually do the right thing once they know
what is right is widespread in our day. It's easy to
understand why people want to think that, because
it is flattering to us to think of ourselves that way.
But the Bible paints a different picture of the state
of the lost. "They are all gone out of the way, they
are together become unprofitable; there is none
that doeth good, no, not one" (Romans 3:12).

Despite the teaching of Scripture that we
receive a new nature upon salvation, some people
seem to want to stay as close to the old nature
as they can rather than walking daily as a new

creation of God. Because He is holy, He requires holy living from us. And because of His power we are no longer in bondage to sin, without the ability to do what is right. Charles Spurgeon said, "The liberty of the man of the world is liberty to commit evil without restraint; the liberty of a child of God is to walk in holiness without hindrance."

We do not work to earn our salvation or merit with God. When we trust Christ as our Savior, He saves us fully and freely. But sometimes we overlook the reality that, as His children who now have been freed from our old bondage to sin, we should desire to walk in a way that is pleasing to the Lord. God gives us the resources we need for this worthy walk, but we must make the choice to use them. There is freedom in Christ, but it is freedom *from* sin, not freedom *to* sin.

The Gospel in You Today

You have the privilege and responsibility to walk in a manner worthy of a child of God.

AN UNBREAKABLE BOND

Nay, in all these things we are more than conquerors through him that loved us. For I am persuaded, that neither death, nor life, nor angels, nor principalities, nor powers, nor things present, nor things to come, Nor height, nor depth, nor any other creature, shall be able to separate us from the love of God, which is in Christ Jesus our Lord.—**Romans 8:37–39**

During World War II while working with a team of scientists to develop new materials for gun sights, Harry Coover, Jr. discovered a substance they named cyanoacrylate. It was unsuitable for their purpose so it was set aside. But a few years later when Coover was working for Eastman Kodak, he came up with a use for cyanoacrylate in a product that almost all of us have used. In 1958, the company began selling an adhesive called Eastman 910, the first commercially available version of what we today commonly call super glue. It stuck to almost any surface, and created a bond that was nearly impossible to break.

God's love for us is an even more powerful adhesive. There is nothing in Heaven or on Earth that can dissolve the bond of that love. The devil comes and tells us that God cannot or will not love us because of what we have done or failed to do. This is a lie. God's love for us is not dependent on us, but is an unchanging part of His nature. "But God commendeth his love toward us, in that, while we were yet sinners, Christ died for us" (Romans 5:8).

Most of us have been disappointed or let down by people we trusted and counted on. Most of us have had people turn against us for one reason or another. God never fails. His love for us is eternal and unchanging—a bond that cannot be broken. We can rely on it because love is who God is.

The Gospel in You Today

You can count on God's unfailing love no matter who or what tries to take it away.

THE PATH TO POWER

*And be found in him, not having mine own righteousness,
which is of the law, but that which is through the faith of
Christ, the righteousness which is of God by faith: That
I may know him, and the power of his resurrection, and
the fellowship of his sufferings, being made conformable
unto his death; If by any means I might attain unto the
resurrection of the dead.*—**Philippians 3:9–11**

Paul met Jesus when he was on the way to
Damascus to persecute Christians there. Paul
was fully aware that Jesus had been crucified, and
that day he became fully aware that Jesus was alive
again. Paul never lost sight of the truth of the
resurrection. He recognized what having the power
over death meant—that there was literally nothing
that could stand against it. Paul devoted his life to
telling others about the risen Lord, working in the
power of the resurrection.

But in writing to the church at Philippi, the
place where, as Acts 16 tells us, he had previously
been beaten and cast into prison while preaching
the gospel, Paul described the path to experiencing

resurrection power. And it is not an easy road. We cannot know resurrection power without first knowing the pain of suffering and death to self. Lester Roloff said, "Nobody ever got resurrected who wasn't dead first." The reason many Christians do not have God's power is that they are not willing to surrender themselves to experience it.

The power of God has not changed or lessened with the passage of years. The Holy Spirit indwells every believer. "But if the Spirit of him that raised up Jesus from the dead dwell in you, he that raised up Christ from the dead shall also quicken your mortal bodies by his Spirit that dwelleth in you" (Romans 8:11). The question is not whether there is power available to meet our needs, but whether we are willing to lay aside whatever is necessary to have it.

The Gospel in You Today

God's resurrection power is available to every Christian who is willing to die to self.

GOD'S PLAN REQUIRES CHANGE

I beseech you therefore, brethren, by the mercies of God, that ye present your bodies a living sacrifice, holy, acceptable unto God, which is your reasonable service. And be not conformed to this world: but be ye transformed by the renewing of your mind, that ye may prove what is that good, and acceptable, and perfect, will of God.
—**Romans 12:1–2**

It is a normal part of human nature to resist change. We see it in families, in churches, in businesses, in politics—all across the board new ideas tend to be met with at least skepticism if not outright rejection. I read about a man who said his doctor had told him to cut red meat out of his diet, and as a result, he had stopped putting ketchup on his hamburgers! Not all resistance to change is bad, because not all change is good. Since the truth never changes, there are things that must not change. But there are some changes that are an integral part of God's plan for our lives.

Christ did not save us for us to stay as we were. "Therefore if any man be in Christ, he is a new creature: old things are passed away; behold, all things are become new" (2 Corinthians 5:17). If nothing is changing, if we are not becoming more and more like Jesus, something is wrong. God's plan is for us to be transformed in His image. Only as we allow Him to change us will we become what He wills for us to be.

The problem often comes when we are reluctant to make a change that we know is necessary for godly living. We easily get attached to our sins and want to hold them fast. We find holiness to be confining, keeping us from pleasures we should not enjoy. Instead we must be willing participants in God's lifelong program to change us to be like Him.

The Gospel in You Today

When you yield to God's plan of change, you will find His will is good, acceptable, and perfect.

POWER DESTROYED

Knowing this, that our old man is crucified with him, that the body of sin might be destroyed, that henceforth we should not serve sin. For he that is dead is freed from sin. Now if we be dead with Christ, we believe that we shall also live with him: Knowing that Christ being raised from the dead dieth no more; death hath no more dominion over him.—**Romans 6:6–9**

Alarmed by the growing threat of Iran's nuclear program, around 2005 (the details have never been released publicly) the American and Israeli intelligence services created a new kind of weapon—a computer "worm." This program worked by making copies of itself over and over on each new computer with which it came in contact. When it had spread, Stuxnet, as the worm was called, began altering the speeds at which the centrifuges used to enrich uranium ran. The program was designed so that the controls would report everything was normal, even as the sensitive equipment was being damaged or destroyed. In the end, Iran still had the buildings and equipment standing, but their power to enrich uranium to create nuclear weapons had been largely taken away.

Before we are saved, we are completely unable to resist the power of sin. No amount of will power or good intentions can deliver a lost person from Satan. Paul described this condition to Timothy: "And that they may recover themselves out of the snare of the devil, who are taken captive by him at his will" (2 Timothy 2:26). But Jesus has, through His death and resurrection, destroyed the power that sin had to control us. The same habits and desires that once held us in captivity are still there after salvation, but they no longer have the ability to force our surrender to evil. Though we still sin, it is no longer because we have no choice, but because we have given in to a powerful foe.

The Gospel in You Today

The dominion of sin over you has been destroyed, and you are no longer forced to yield to it.

Day
67

CHOOSING YOUR RULER

Let not sin therefore reign in your mortal body, that ye should obey it in the lusts thereof. Neither yield ye your members as instruments of unrighteousness unto sin: but yield yourselves unto God, as those that are alive from the dead, and your members as instruments of righteousness unto God. For sin shall not have dominion over you: for ye are not under the law, but under grace.
—**Romans 6:12–14**

The sixteenth and seventeenth centuries in England were marked by frequent wars over religious disputes. After Henry VIII established the Church of England, there was a struggle between Catholics and the new church for control of the government. The issue was thought to be settled by the late 1600s, but when the Catholic James II was placed on the throne after the death of his brother, the people feared a renewed conflict. To prevent that, the "Glorious Revolution," as it came to be known, installed the Dutch King William of Orange on England's throne as King William III.

THE GOSPEL IN YOU

William ensured that Catholic control of England would not return. Today in the United States, we have the opportunity to elect representative leaders on a regular basis. In so doing, we are choosing those who will lead us.

There is a similar principle at work in our spiritual lives. No one has the option of being an independent ruler of his own life. Everyone serves something or someone. Some people allow sin to rule over them, obeying what Satan wants rather than what God says. Some people allow God to rule over them, denying the lusts and desires that once motivated their actions. Even after we are saved, we still face temptation to sin and struggle against the flesh. But sin no longer has the power to compel us to do evil. The only way we return to its grasp is if we choose for sin to rule over us again.

The Gospel in You Today

Everyone is ruled by something—it is your choice whether your ruler is God or sin.

DON'T GO BACK TO THE DARK

But God be thanked, that ye were the servants of sin, but ye have obeyed from the heart that form of doctrine which was delivered you. Being then made free from sin, ye became the servants of righteousness. I speak after the manner of men because of the infirmity of your flesh: for as ye have yielded your members servants to uncleanness and to iniquity unto iniquity; even so now yield your members servants to righteousness unto holiness.
—**Romans 6:17–19**

In April of 2006, two workers were trapped in a gold mine near Beaconsfield, Australia, after an earthquake caused the tunnels to collapse. They only survived because they were able to make it into a safety cage that kept them from being crushed by falling rocks. For five days no one outside the mine knew whether they had survived. Finally a thermal imaging scan revealed their location, and rescue efforts began. It was a full fourteen days before rescuers could create a shaft large enough for the miners to escape. The head of the miner's union called the rescue a "great escape."

All of us are born trapped as slaves to sin. There is no hope that we can rescue ourselves. Unless someone comes from the outside to help, we are doomed. That is what Jesus did for us on the cross. We who have received Him as our Savior have been freed from the power that sin once had over our lives. Yet if we're honest, we must admit that even after we are saved, the allure of sin remains. And it will as long as we live in this fallen world.

Having been freed from our captivity, we must resist the temptation to crawl back into the darkness of sin. Paul wrote, "Stand fast therefore in the liberty wherewith Christ hath made us free, and be not entangled again with the yoke of bondage" (Galatians 5:1).

The Gospel in You Today

When you sin, you are willingly exchanging freedom and light for slavery and darkness.

GIVEN ACCESS

Wherefore remember, that ye being in time past Gentiles in the flesh, who are called Uncircumcision by that which is called the Circumcision in the flesh made by hands; That at that time ye were without Christ, being aliens from the commonwealth of Israel, and strangers from the covenants of promise, having no hope, and without God in the world: But now in Christ Jesus ye who sometimes were far off are made nigh by the blood of Christ.
—**Ephesians 2:11–13**

From the beginning of Creation, God had perfect fellowship with man. But when Adam sinned, that fellowship was broken. No longer did Adam look forward to spending time with God, but in shame hid himself. Since that time, sin has continued to stand as a barrier between God and men. Nothing we can do could reach across that divide.

> Not the labor of my hands
> Can fulfill Thy law's demands;
> Could my zeal no respite know,
> Could my tears forever flow,

THE GOSPEL IN YOU

All for sin could not atone;
Thou must save, and Thou alone.
—Augustus Toplady, in "Rock of Ages"

What we could never do, Jesus did for us. His death and resurrection made salvation possible. It also places us into God's family, giving us full access to God. "By whom also we have access by faith into this grace wherein we stand, and rejoice in hope of the glory of God" (Romans 5:2). Jesus shed His precious blood to bring us back into fellowship with God. Yet like spoiled children, many times we ignore the amazing grace and love of our Father, and neglect to spend time with Him. Given access to a close fellowship with God, instead we choose to fill our hearts and minds with frivolous or even sinful things. Salvation offers us fellowship, but we must choose to live in it.

The Gospel in You Today

The access you have to God is a precious treasure;
take advantage of it.

EXPOSING SIN

What shall we say then? Is the law sin? God forbid. Nay, I had not known sin, but by the law: for I had not known lust, except the law had said, Thou shalt not covet. But sin, taking occasion by the commandment, wrought in me all manner of concupiscence. For without the law sin was dead. For I was alive without the law once: but when the commandment came, sin revived, and I died. And the commandment, which was ordained to life, I found to be unto death.—**Romans 7:7–10**

If you've ever done a home improvement project that involved painting, you know how important light is to getting the job done right. In a dim light, your paint job looks quite different than it does in the bright sunshine. It is easy to miss spots and think you have done a good job until the light shines on it. The same thing is true for cleaning. Dust hides in darkness, but the light reveals. The light does not make the dirt; it simply exposes it. And that is why people respond so negatively to having the truth of God's Word brought to bear on their sin. "And this is the condemnation, that light is come into the world, and men loved darkness rather than light, because their deeds were evil" (John 3:19).

What is true of the lost can be true of Christians as well. If we are drawing away from close fellowship with other believers and spending less time in the Bible, it is an indication that something is wrong in our hearts. God uses His Word—and specifically the law—to reveal our sin to us. If we are trying to avoid the light, there is likely something in our lives that we are hoping to conceal.

God does not want our sin to remain hidden, and the Holy Spirit will send lights—whether through His Word directly, from other Christians, or by circumstances—to expose what we are attempting to conceal from Him and from others.

The Gospel in You Today

The only cure for sinful living is exposure to the light that leads us to repentance.

STANDING ON A ROCK

I waited patiently for the LORD; and he inclined unto me, and heard my cry. He brought me up also out of an horrible pit, out of the miry clay, and set my feet upon a rock, and established my goings. And he hath put a new song in my mouth, even praise unto our God: many shall see it, and fear, and shall trust in the LORD.
—**Psalm 40:1–3**

Charles Spurgeon told of an elderly Welsh lady who was visited by a preacher as she lay on her deathbed. He asked if she were sinking, and she just looked at him. He repeated the question, and she continued her silence. When he asked the third time she raised herself up a little and said, "Sinking! Sinking! Did you ever know a sinner to sink through a rock? If I had been standing on the sand, I might sink; but thank God, I'm on the Rock of Ages, and there is no sinking there."

Because our salvation is all God's doing and not our own responsibility, we do not need to worry if we are secure in Him. He not only does all the saving, but all the keeping as well. Jesus said of those who belong to Him, "And I give unto them eternal life; and they shall never perish, neither shall any man pluck them out of my hand" (John 10:28). He is an unfailing, unchanging Rock, and we can have full confidence in Him. There are few more effective tools of the devil than to get us focused on ourselves rather than on God. He is the one we can trust both to take us to Heaven and to guide and provide for us here on Earth.

David said that God "established my goings." That did not mean David had an easy life. What it meant was that God was the rock David could trust no matter what circumstances might come. God was just as present with David when he was running for his life as when he was sitting in the palace. God never changes, and He never breaks a promise.

The Gospel in You Today

Because God is your rock, your trust in Him for salvation—as well as every other aspect of your life—is well placed.

THE WILLING SACRIFICE

As the Father knoweth me, even so know I the Father:
and I lay down my life for the sheep. And other sheep I
have, which are not of this fold: them also I must bring,
and they shall hear my voice; and there shall be one
fold, and one shepherd. Therefore doth my Father love
me, because I lay down my life, that I might take it again.
No man taketh it from me, but I lay it down of myself. I
have power to lay it down, and I have power to take it
again. This commandment have I received of my Father.
—**John 10:15–18**

Thomas Piggott went to China in 1879 as a missionary to work with Hudson Taylor in reaching the lost. In May of 1896, he wrote: "How shall we look on the investment of our lives and labour here, even from the near standpoint of one hundred years hence? I am, I can truly say, more grateful every day for the opportunity of serving Christ, and I believe this to be the only true and sober view of life's realities. The work pressed home now, will make all the difference a few years hence." When the Boxer Rebellion broke out, Piggott refused to leave and was executed along with dozens of other missionaries. He gave his life for the gospel.

The apostle Paul grounded his appeal for Christians to willingly serve God on the sacrifice that Jesus made for our salvation. "I beseech you therefore, brethren, by the mercies of God, that ye present your bodies a living sacrifice, holy, acceptable unto God, which is your reasonable service" (Romans 12:1). Jesus was not dragged to the cross by forces beyond His control. He willingly laid down His life for us, and He calls us to do the same for others. "Hereby perceive we the love of God, because he laid down his life for us: and we ought to lay down our lives for the brethren" (1 John 3:16).

The Gospel in You Today

Because of what Jesus willingly gave for you, be willing to sacrifice for Him and for others.

CHILDREN OF GOD

For ye have not received the spirit of bondage again to fear; but ye have received the Spirit of adoption, whereby we cry, Abba, Father. The Spirit itself beareth witness with our spirit, that we are the children of God: And if children, then heirs; heirs of God, and joint-heirs with Christ; if so be that we suffer with him, that we may be also glorified together.—**Romans 8:15–17**

Most children in our society grow up learning to talk from their parents. So it's no surprise that for many the first word is either "Mama" or "Dada." It is an early expression of a relationship that will grow and develop over the years. These words, even in their simple forms, convey great meaning. They speak of love and trust and kinship. It is this two-syllable Dada that is similar to the Hebrew Abba that we are allowed to use in addressing God because He has made us His children through salvation. "Behold, what manner of love the Father hath bestowed upon us, that we should be called the sons of God: therefore the world knoweth us not, because it knew him not" (1 John 3:1).

We would never think of walking into a stranger's house at mealtime and sitting down at the table, expecting to be served a meal. We have no relationship with him and no reason to expect him to respond to us. But when we approach God, we are walking into the presence of our Father. And while He is a high and holy God to be worshiped and feared, He is also our Abba who loves us deeply. Dr. Bob Jones Sr. said that prayer for our needs to be met was like sitting down at the dinner table and saying, "Pappy, please pass the biscuits." We do not treat God flippantly or casually, but we do have the right to boldly enter the presence of our Heavenly Father, and He encourages us to do so.

"He that spared not his own Son, but delivered him up for us all, how shall he not with him also freely give us all things?" (Romans 8:32).

The Gospel in You Today

Never lose sight of the amazing love your Father in Heaven has for you.

THE POWER OF SCRIPTURE

And when the tempter came to him, he said, If thou be the
Son of God, command that these stones be made bread.
But he answered and said, It is written, Man shall not live
by bread alone, but by every word that proceedeth out of
the mouth of God.—**Matthew 4:3–4**

Long before Israel ever had a king, God gave
Moses instructions for how those who
would lead His people should live. One of the
requirements was for the king to write out a copy
of the Law, which he would keep and read day
after day (Deuteronomy 17:18–19). That would
have been a laborious and time-intensive process,
requiring commitment and diligence. This
devotion to Scripture was the key to the king's
obedience to God's commands. They needed to be
known, repeatedly read, and daily emphasized so
that they would be followed.

I remember the first Bible I was ever given.
Inside the front cover were written these words:
"Sin will keep you from this book, or this book will

keep you from sin." The Bible is a source of power given to us through which we can triumph over temptation and sin. That's why the psalmist said, "Thy word have I hid in mine heart, that I might not sin against thee" (Psalm 119:11). And it is why Jesus, when He was tempted by the devil, quoted Scripture to defeat that temptation. Each time Jesus said, "It is written..." He followed by quoting from the Old Testament Scriptures.

John tells us, "For whatsoever is born of God overcometh the world: and this is the victory that overcometh the world, even our faith" (1 John 5:4). Paul gives us the source of faith, "So then faith cometh by hearing, and hearing by the word of God" (Romans 10:17). Knowledge and diligent use of God's Word is the best protection we have against temptation.

The Gospel in You Today

Don't try to defeat temptation in your own strength, but use the powerful Word of God.

THE QUEST FOR PEACE

Let not then your good be evil spoken of: For the kingdom of God is not meat and drink; but righteousness, and peace, and joy in the Holy Ghost. For he that in these things serveth Christ is acceptable to God, and approved of men. Let us therefore follow after the things which make for peace, and things wherewith one may edify another.—**Romans 14:16–19**

At the 1972 Olympics in Munich, the long-distance runners from Finland, the "Flying Finns," were expected to do well. But on the twelfth lap of the 10,000 meter race, their favorite, Lassie Viren, collided with another runner and fell to the track. Undaunted, he got up and began chasing the runners ahead of him. Incredibly, he not only caught up with the field, but passed them. Viren won the first of his four gold medals while setting a new world record despite the fall. He chased down the field, exerting all of his strength to catch up.

That is an illustration of what Paul was talking about in Romans 14 where he instructs us to "follow after" peace. This is not a casual, occasional, conditional following. Instead it is a full effort, expending whatever is required in order to catch up with peace. Peace is hard to come by in our world, whether between nations, people groups, political parties, or even families. Too often, peace is hard to come by even in our churches.

Each of us has the responsibility to do whatever we can, without violating biblical principles, to promote peace. Instead of waiting for someone else to take the first step, we should follow the instructions of Romans 12:18: "If it be possible, as much as lieth in you, live peaceably with all men." The only way we will exert the proper effort toward peace is if we value it highly. When we grasp the high value God places on His children getting along, we will work diligently toward that goal.

The Gospel in You Today

The best way to have peace with brothers and sisters in Christ is to take responsibility to put forth effort toward ensuring it exists.

REMEMBER AND REPENT

And unto the angel of the church in Sardis write; These things saith he that hath the seven Spirits of God, and the seven stars; I know thy works, that thou hast a name that thou livest, and art dead. Be watchful, and strengthen the things which remain, that are ready to die: for I have not found thy works perfect before God. Remember therefore how thou hast received and heard, and hold fast, and repent. If therefore thou shalt not watch, I will come on thee as a thief, and thou shalt not know what hour I will come upon thee.—**Revelation 3:1–3**

Many times when we think about remembrance in terms of repentance, we think of guilt and shame and sorrow for past transgressions. While godly sorrow is important, we must be careful not to be bound by the past. We cannot change it, and if we have confessed and forsaken sin and done what we can to make things right with anyone we harmed, we should let the past go. But there is another kind of remembrance that promotes repentance—the memory of the good things God has given to and done for us. "Or despisest thou the riches of his goodness and forbearance and longsuffering; not knowing that the goodness of God leadeth thee to repentance?" (Romans 2:4).

When we forget what God has done, we are vulnerable to temptation. And if we continue forgetting, we are slow to repent and confess our sins.

God is always good to us. This is just as true when things are going poorly by our judgment as it is when things are going well. Sometimes people even excuse their sin by citing what they view as a failure on God's part. If we stop to reflect on His perfect love and the sweetness of close fellowship with Him, we will quickly turn away from our sin and repent.

The Gospel in You Today

Allow God's goodness to cause you to quickly seek restored fellowship with Him when you sin.

A PASSION FOR THE LOST

For I will not dare to speak of any of those things which Christ hath not wrought by me, to make the Gentiles obedient, by word and deed, Through mighty signs and wonders, by the power of the Spirit of God; so that from Jerusalem, and round about unto Illyricum, I have fully preached the gospel of Christ. Yea, so have I strived to preach the gospel, not where Christ was named, lest I should build upon another man's foundation: But as it is written, To whom he was not spoken of, they shall see: and they that have not heard shall understand.
—**Romans 15:18–21**

The Roman Empire in the days of Paul was huge, stretching across most of Europe as well as parts of Africa and Asia. Paul took advantage of his status as a full Roman citizen and used the network of roads built by the empire to travel across much of it preaching the gospel. His vision and passion was to go to places where the news of the Savior had not yet reached, and it was to that cause he devoted so much of his life.

THE GOSPEL IN YOU

In our day with modern communication technology, we tend to think that the gospel is already everywhere—that there are no places where Christ is not named. But in truth there are still many nations and people groups with no clear gospel witness. This ought to concern all of us who are Christians, for it is our responsibility to change it. Paul wrote, "Awake to righteousness, and sin not; for some have not the knowledge of God: I speak this to your shame" (1 Corinthians 15:34).

Even in America where there are many churches, there are still many people who have never heard a clear and personal presentation of the gospel. Between the false teachings that are so popular and those who ignore or oppose all religions, there is much confusion we must counter with the truth.

The Gospel in You Today

We need a renewed passion and sense of urgency for reaching the lost with the gospel.

THE HELP WE DON'T EVEN KNOW WE NEED

Likewise the Spirit also helpeth our infirmities: for we know not what we should pray for as we ought: but the Spirit itself maketh intercession for us with groanings which cannot be uttered. And he that searcheth the hearts knoweth what is the mind of the Spirit, because he maketh intercession for the saints according to the will of God. And we know that all things work together for good to them that love God, to them who are the called according to his purpose.—**Romans 8:26–28**

Every child of God receives the Holy Spirit at the moment of salvation. This indwelling is not something we have to go back and get later or only receive after some additional spiritual experience. It is immediate. And while we do not always walk in the Spirit, He is always there with us. "What? know ye not that your body is the temple of the Holy Ghost which is in you, which ye have of God, and ye are not your own?" (1 Corinthians 6:19).

THE GOSPEL IN YOU

The Holy Spirit is sent to encourage us and ensure our salvation, but He is also sent to guide us. This is not a mystical guidance that depends on the shape of clouds or the meaning of dreams, but it is a guidance based on the Word of God as the Holy Spirit who inspired the writers helps us understand and apply His truth to our lives.

Sometimes we forget how desperately we need the Holy Spirit's help. Paul tells us that when we don't even know how or what we should pray for, the Holy Spirit intercedes for us. Most of us have had the experience of looking back at something we wanted and prayed for, sometimes quite fervently, only to later realize that not getting it was a true blessing. Rather than insisting on our own way—in prayer or in any other aspect of life—we should remember the compassionate care of the Holy Spirit and accept the help He provides.

The Gospel in You Today

Rely on the Holy Spirit's help for your daily growth.

THE DEVIL'S ATTEMPT TO DIVIDE

Who shall lay any thing to the charge of God's elect? It is God that justifieth. Who is he that condemneth? It is Christ that died, yea rather, that is risen again, who is even at the right hand of God, who also maketh intercession for us. Who shall separate us from the love of Christ? shall tribulation, or distress, or persecution, or famine, or nakedness, or peril, or sword?—**Romans 8:33–35**

Ever since the Garden of Eden, Satan has been working to separate people from God. He knows that the closer we are to the Lord, the less power he has in our lives. That is one reason so many Christians endure tribulation, distress, and persecution. The devil is trying to do to them the same thing that he tried to do to Job—to separate them from God, undermine their faith, and render them ineffective in service to Him.

e possibilities for trouble and even
ution are real. I have talked to people who
een put in jail for their faith. I have talked to
wed spouses of those who were killed for their

faith. I have seen the pain and sorrow these attacks bring. They are not figments of the imagination. They are not easy to face, but they are utterly incapable of changing God's love for us. We can allow them to defeat us, but that is not a failure on God's part.

When trouble comes, it should drive us closer to God rather than further away from Him. David wrote, "In the LORD put I my trust: how say ye to my soul, Flee as a bird to your mountain?" (Psalm 11:1). No human refuge can fully sustain us in trials. There is no fortress that can protect us. Only God can overcome the power of the devil. Our responsibility is to maintain our relationship with Him, trusting in His love just as much when things go wrong as when they go right.

The Gospel in You Today

Do not let anything that happens shake your faith in God's unfailing love for you.

CONQUERING LOVE

Nay, in all these things we are more than conquerors through him that loved us. For I am persuaded, that neither death, nor life, nor angels, nor principalities, nor powers, nor things present, nor things to come, Nor height, nor depth, nor any other creature, shall be able to separate us from the love of God, which is in Christ Jesus our Lord.—**Romans 8:37–39**

I read about a missionary to Zimbabwe who was trying to hand out copies of the New Testament in the local language. One man was resistant to receiving it, finally telling the missionary that if he did take it, he would use the pages of Scripture to wrap his tobacco to smoke. The missionary said, "At least read each page before you burn it." Fifteen years passed, and that same man came up to the missionary at a conference. The man had not only been saved, but he was now a full-time evangelist. He explained, "I smoked through Matthew. I smoked through Mark. I smoked through Luke. But when I got to John 3:16, I couldn't smoke any more!"

The love of God never falters. Human relationships, even the closest relationships, may be broken. David wrote, "When my father and my mother forsake me, then the Lord will take me up" (Psalm 27:10).

It is hard for us to comprehend unfailing love, because it is not natural. We cannot look around us and see examples of it in people, or even in ourselves. All of us are limited, but God is not. He is eternal, and because of His nature, He never surrenders His love. "Now before the feast of the passover, when Jesus knew that his hour was come that he should depart out of this world unto the Father, having loved his own which were in the world, he loved them unto the end" (John 13:1). It is in that unfailing love that we can confidently face every challenge.

The Gospel in You Today

God's love to you, expressed through
the gift of His Son, never fails.

FIRST THINGS FIRST

He saith unto them, Come and see. They came and saw where he dwelt, and abode with him that day: for it was about the tenth hour. One of the two which heard John speak, and followed him, was Andrew, Simon Peter's brother. He first findeth his own brother Simon, and saith unto him, We have found the Messias, which is, being interpreted, the Christ. And he brought him to Jesus. And when Jesus beheld him, he said, Thou art Simon the son of Jona: thou shalt be called Cephas, which is by interpretation, A stone.—**John 1:39–42**

The Bible tells us that Andrew was a disciple of John the Baptist. We don't know how long he had been following John before Jesus came to be baptized, but the next day Andrew began following Jesus instead. The first thing Andrew did when they reached their destination was to go and find his brother Peter and bring him to Jesus. That was the most important thing he could do, so Andrew did not allow anything to take precedence over that task.

All of us have friends, family members, co-workers, neighbors, and acquaintances who need to know Jesus. And it is our responsibility to introduce them to Him. Not all of them will respond to the gospel, just as not everyone Jesus Himself talked to accepted Him as their Messiah and Savior. But if we do not tell them the truth, where will they hear it? "How then shall they call on him in whom they have not believed? and how shall they believe in him of whom they have not heard? and how shall they hear without a preacher?" (Romans 10:14).

We need a renewed sense of urgency and priority when it comes to reaching people with the gospel. It is right for us to send and support missionaries to other places. But we have a responsibility to those around us to be a witness.

The Gospel in You Today

There are many good things you can
and should do, but none are more important
than bringing people to Jesus.

NOT ASHAMED

Whereunto I am appointed a preacher, and an apostle, and a teacher of the Gentiles. For the which cause I also suffer these things: nevertheless I am not ashamed: for I know whom I have believed, and am persuaded that he is able to keep that which I have committed unto him against that day. Hold fast the form of sound words, which thou hast heard of me, in faith and love which is in Christ Jesus.—2 **Timothy** 1:11-13

Paul would have had a much easier life if he had simply kept quiet about his encounter with Jesus on the road to Damascus. If he had never told anyone what happened, he would not have suffered so much—running for his life, being imprisoned, beaten, whipped, and stoned. He would not have been jailed in Rome before being executed. But despite all that he endured, Paul was not silent as long as he lived. He would not stop talking about Jesus. Even before he made his trip to Rome in chains, Paul wrote, "So, as much as in me is, I am ready to preach the gospel to you that are at Rome also" (Romans 1:15).

THE GOSPEL IN YOU

There are things for which people should be ashamed. In our day many of those things are now being praised by the society around us. We should never take part in anything of which we legitimately would be ashamed. But we should never be ashamed when we are judged or condemned or criticized or even persecuted for doing and saying what is right.

The world may not accept the truth. They may mock and scorn us. And they may exact economic hardship or even worse. But we should never be ashamed of the truth or of the Lord who saved us. Instead, we should do all we can to share the message of the gospel with a world desperately in need of it.

The Gospel in You Today

Our commitment to Christ should be
so strong that we are not ashamed of any
suffering that follows from it.

JOY IN HARD TIMES

And not only so, but we glory in tribulations also: knowing that tribulation worketh patience; And patience, experience; and experience, hope: And hope maketh not ashamed; because the love of God is shed abroad in our hearts by the Holy Ghost which is given unto us.
—**Romans 5:3–5**

Our attitudes are not determined by our circumstances. Some people are joyful during times of great trial. Others are discontent even in times of plenty. Our attitudes are determined by our view of those circumstances. If we view hard times as unfair or surprising, we will likely allow them to drag us down. If, on the other hand, we view hard times as part of God's purpose for our lives, we will keep our joy.

Nothing ever takes God by surprise. We may be blindsided by things we didn't see coming, but God never is. And while there are times when His plan involves us going through great hardship and trial, there is never a time when we get there accidentally. Our hardships are opportunities for our faith to grow and God's power to be displayed. Writing to people who were experiencing intense persecution for their faith, Peter said, "But rejoice, inasmuch as ye are partakers of Christ's sufferings; that, when his glory shall be revealed, ye may be glad also with exceeding joy" (1 Peter 4:13).

In the allegorical book *Pilgrim's Progress,* when the characters Christian and Hopeful were trapped in Doubting Castle by the Giant Despair, they spent days in a basement prison. Finally, Christian remembered something important. "'What a fool,' quoth he, 'am I, thus to lie in a stinking dungeon, when I may as well walk at liberty! I have a key in my bosom called Promise; that will, I am persuaded, open any lock in Doubting Castle.'" The key worked, and the two walked free rejoicing to continue on to the Celestial City.

The Gospel in You Today

Because of God's promises, you can be joyful in the most difficult circumstances.

ABOUNDING HOPE

And again, Esaias saith, There shall be a root of Jesse, and he that shall rise to reign over the Gentiles; in him shall the Gentiles trust. Now the God of hope fill you with all joy and peace in believing, that ye may abound in hope, through the power of the Holy Ghost. And I myself also am persuaded of you, my brethren, that ye also are full of goodness, filled with all knowledge, able also to admonish one another.—**Romans 15:12–14**

After more than two decades of faithful ministry and service to God, Thomas Brooks faced a crisis. The Church of England in 1662 persuaded Parliament to pass a law called the Act of Uniformity. This required all preachers to give an oath to follow the Book of Common Prayer or lose their positions. More than 2,500 ministers, including Brooks, refused and were ousted in what came to be called the Great Ejection. Thomas Brooks said, "Hope can see Heaven through the thickest clouds."

While all of us would prefer to experience calm and peace, the reality is that being faithful to God may place us in difficult situations and cost us a great deal. Many through the years have had friends turn against them because of a stand for the truth. But even if taking a stand costs us everything we have in earthly terms, we are not left alone and hopeless.

God is the God of hope, and He can and does work through any circumstances to accomplish His purposes. If we look to ourselves for strength, we will surely be discouraged and disappointed. But when we look to the God of hope and walk in the Spirit, nothing can take that hope away. God's plan for our lives is not merely a little hope, but a hope that abounds and overcomes fear and doubt so that we will be faithful to Him in every situation.

The Gospel in You Today

As long as God lives, and He lives forever, you are never abandoned or hopeless—no matter what happens.

WHERE THE BATTLE IS WON OR LOST

And he went a little further, and fell on his face, and prayed, saying, O my Father, if it be possible, let this cup pass from me: nevertheless not as I will, but as thou wilt. And he cometh unto the disciples, and findeth them asleep, and saith unto Peter, What, could ye not watch with me one hour? Watch and pray, that ye enter not into temptation: the spirit indeed is willing, but the flesh is weak.—**Matthew 26:39–41**

The Duke of Wellington commanded the British armies at one of the most famous battles in all of history, Waterloo. There Napoleon was defeated for a second time and removed from power for good. The "Iron Duke" was revered throughout England following that victory, and was often asked to attend public ceremonies and dedications. Some ten years after the Battle of Waterloo, Wellington returned to Eton College, where he had once been a student. Watching a cricket match between students, Wellington remarked, "The battle of Waterloo was won here." He recognized that the lessons young men learned while in school, long before they ever faced battle, had carried over to the battlefield and made a crucial difference there.

The time to resist temptation is not when it appears, but long before. Jesus warned Peter that Satan was going to be making a special effort to tempt him, but Peter did not take the warning seriously. When it was time to pray, he was sleeping. It is of little surprise, then, when we read that he quickly denied even knowing Jesus let alone being one of His disciples (Matthew 26:69–75). If we are on guard, alert, and praying, temptation becomes much less effective. Though none of us will ever be sinless in this life, we can and will sin less if we prepare to resist temptation before it even approaches us. God's overcoming power is released into our lives as we seek Him in prayer.

The Gospel in You Today

Be faithful in prayer so you will be strong to resist temptation.

KEEPING AN EYE ON THE REAL ENEMY

For, brethren, ye have been called unto liberty; only use not liberty for an occasion to the flesh, but by love serve one another. For all the law is fulfilled in one word, even in this; Thou shalt love thy neighbour as thyself. But if ye bite and devour one another, take heed that ye be not consumed one of another.—**Galatians 5:13–15**

In the late 1800s, a civil war in the Samoan Islands sparked international worry. The various world powers that had influence in the region feared the loss of their preferred status so they backed different sides in the conflict. Warships from Germany, Great Britain, and the United States converged on Samoa. They remained in a standoff in Apia Harbor, unwilling to actually fight, but also unwilling to leave and allow another nation to gain influence. The standoff continued for weeks until a massive cyclone wrecked all six warships in the harbor. The power of the wind and waves didn't care about the different sides or their opinions, but equally struck them all.

THE GOSPEL IN YOU

As Christians, we have a real enemy to fight. "Be sober, be vigilant; because your adversary the devil, as a roaring lion, walketh about, seeking whom he may devour" (1 Peter 5:8). We must never shirk from standing for the truth and doing what is right, even if it requires a battle. But there are other battles that simply serve to distract us from the real enemy, and we must not fight these. A division or conflict that arises because of a stand for truth is different from one that arises because of pride or personality clashes. Without changing our biblical convictions, we should make every effort to avoid conflict with other Christians. "If it be possible, as much as lieth in you, live peaceably with all men" (Romans 12:18). Our strength should be devoted to fighting against the devil.

The Gospel in You Today

We should never allow personal conflict
to divide us from Christians who are
committed to following Christ.

NO CONDEMNATION

There is therefore now no condemnation to them which are in Christ Jesus, who walk not after the flesh, but after the Spirit. For the law of the Spirit of life in Christ Jesus hath made me free from the law of sin and death. For what the law could not do, in that it was weak through the flesh, God sending his own Son in the likeness of sinful flesh, and for sin, condemned sin in the flesh: That the righteousness of the law might be fulfilled in us, who walk not after the flesh, but after the Spirit.—**Romans 8:1–4**

In March of 2019, Harry Krame returned a book to the library in Fair Lawn, New Jersey. People return books to the public library every day. But what made this return noteworthy was that Krame had checked out *The Family Book of Verse* by Lewis Ganet when Lyndon B. Johnson was president—fifty-three years before he returned it. The book had been stacked with others and stored in his basement. When Krame found the book during a cleanup, he said he felt guilty for keeping it so long. Though the fine would have amounted to some $2,000, the library waived all the fees and said they would use the book as part of an exhibit to stress the importance of returning library books on time.

There are things in the past of all of our lives that we look back on with regret. Poor decisions, harsh words, failed efforts, and especially sin (both of omission and commission). Yet while we should never take sin lightly, we should also not be bound by guilt over what God has forgiven. Once we have confessed a sin and forsaken it, and done what we can to make things right with those we have hurt, the sin is gone. God does not bring forgiven sin up again, and neither should we. "As far as the east is from the west, so far hath he removed our transgressions from us." "For I will be merciful to their unrighteousness, and their sins and their iniquities will I remember no more" (Psalm 103:12, Hebrews 8:12).

The Gospel in You Today

Salvation freed you from the guilt, shame, and condemnation of the past forever.

KILLING SELF-RIGHTEOUSNESS

But what things were gain to me, those I counted loss for Christ. Yea doubtless, and I count all things but loss for the excellency of the knowledge of Christ Jesus my Lord: for whom I have suffered the loss of all things, and do count them but dung, that I may win Christ, And be found in him, not having mine own righteousness, which is of the law, but that which is through the faith of Christ, the righteousness which is of God by faith:
—**Philippians 3:7–9**

There is a great temptation facing Christians who have been saved and are serving God faithfully to begin to focus on themselves rather than on God. It is easy to begin to rely on our own strength to win the battles we face. The victories of the past, however, were not won in our power, and if we allow ourselves to take credit for them, glorifying our own righteousness rather than God's, we are on the path to failure and defeat. If we are found with only our own righteousness, we are doomed.

The very best we can accomplish falls far short of God's standard of perfection. A. J. Gordon wrote, "There is nothing of ours, soul, body, or spirit, that is without blemish. And when we understand that our very tears need themselves to be washed in the blood of the Redeemer, and our very penitence to be sanctified in his exceeding sorrow, we shall gladly turn wholly to the perfect offering." The devil whispers in our ear that we can do it on our own, relying on our strength and goodness. Like Samson after his hair was cut, we go out expecting victory because of what "we" have done in the past without regard to God's role, only to be utterly defeated. Victories of the past do not provide protection in future attacks, and if we lean on our own goodness, victory will quickly turn to defeat.

The Gospel in You Today

When we rest in our righteousness, we fall to pride, but when we rest in the perfect righteousness of Christ, we are free to fully depend upon God.

BE PREPARED

Behold, what manner of love the Father hath bestowed upon us, that we should be called the sons of God: therefore the world knoweth us not, because it knew him not. Beloved, now are we the sons of God, and it doth not yet appear what we shall be: but we know that, when he shall appear, we shall be like him; for we shall see him as he is. And every man that hath this hope in him purifieth himself, even as he is pure.—1 **John 3:1–3**

If you were old enough at the time, you remember the Y2K scare. In the late 1990s, people began worrying that computers were not properly programmed to handle dates in the new millennium and would crash. Many warned of electrical outages, banking failures, water shortages, and massive trouble as every computer in the nation might crash at once. People began stockpiling food, medical supplies, and water. Like many families, we filled the bathtubs with water on New Year's Eve, just in case. But in the end, nothing happened. The new millennium rolled in uneventfully.

Why did so many people put so much time, effort, and money into preparing for Y2K? Because they thought that there was at least a chance that things would go wrong, and they wanted to be ready. As Christians, we can know one thing about the future with absolute certainty: Jesus is going to return. Surprisingly, however, many Christians are not living as if they expect Christ to come.

If we do not prepare for the day of the Lord, it indicates that we do not truly believe that day is coming—or at least that we are not anticipating it. While we may not say that out loud, our actions speak loudly that we are not serious about the day when we will see Jesus. If we take His promise to heart, we will prepare for the certainty of His return. "So then every one of us shall give account of himself to God" (Romans 14:12).

The Gospel in You Today

Look with anticipation today toward that wonderful day when you see Christ face to face.

YOU ARE AN EXAMPLE

And ye became followers of us, and of the Lord, having received the word in much affliction, with joy of the Holy Ghost: So that ye were ensamples to all that believe in Macedonia and Achaia. For from you sounded out the word of the Lord not only in Macedonia and Achaia, but also in every place your faith to God-ward is spread abroad; so that we need not to speak any thing.
—1 Thessalonians 1:6–8

It is said that on one occasion someone approached the evangelist George Whitefield and said, "I should like to hear your dying testimony." Whitefield responded, "No, I shall in all probability bear no dying testimony." Somewhat startled, his questioner asked, "Why not?" Whitefield said, "Because I am bearing testimony every day while I live, and there will be the less need of it when I die."

Every day we are setting an example for others, whether we are aware of it or not. When Paul wrote to the church at Thessalonica he told them that he was using them as an example to other believers—

and that even before he did, word of their faith had already spread.

There should be no doubt in the minds of anyone who knows us that we are committed to following God and that He is at work in our lives. While we do not live for the praise or approval of others, we also must not neglect the impact that our lives have on them. Paul wrote, "For none of us liveth to himself, and no man dieth to himself" (Romans 14:7). Every day in ways both large and small, and often in ways we are not even aware of ourselves, we are influencing others. Whether that influence is positive or negative is determined by how closely we are walking with God and allowing His ongoing work of grace to continue in our lives. Always remember that as the gospel transforms *you*, it has an impact on others as well.

The Gospel in You Today

The awareness of our impact on others should remind us to live faithfully each day.

INDEXES

TITLE INDEX

SCRIPTURE INDEX

ABOUT THE AUTHOR

Dr. Paul Chappell is the senior pastor of Lancaster Baptist Church and the president of West Coast Baptist College in Lancaster, California. He is a powerful communicator of God's Word and a passionate servant to God's people. Dr. Chappell and his wife Terrie have been married for over forty years, and they have four married children who are all serving in Christian ministry with their spouses. He enjoys spending time with his family and serving the Lord with a wonderful church family.

Dr. Chappell's preaching is heard on *Daily in the Word*, a radio program that is broadcast across America. You can find a station listing at dailyintheword.org.

You can also connect with Dr. Chappell here:

Blog: paulchappell.com
Twitter: twitter.com/paulchappell
Facebook: facebook.com/pastor.paul.chappell
Instagram: instagram.com/paulchappell